BASIC/NOT BORING LANGUAGE SKILLS

MIDDLE GRADE BOOK OF LANGUAGE TESTS

Series Concept & Development
by Imogene Forte & Marjorie Frank

Illustrations by Kathleen Bullock

Incentive Publications, Inc.
Nashville, Tennessee

About the cover:
Bound resist, or tie dye, is the most ancient known method of fabric surface design. The brilliance of the basic tie dye design on this cover reflects the possibilities that emerge from the mastery of basic skills.

Cover art by Mary Patricia Deprez, dba Tye Dye Mary®
Cover design by Marta Drayton and Joe Shibley
Edited by Angela Reiner

ISBN 0-86530-481-5

PRINTED IN THE UNITED STATES OF AMERICA
www.incentivepublications.com

TABLE OF CONTENTS

INSIDE THE
MIDDLE GRADE BOOK OF LANGUAGE TESTS

"I wish I had a convenient, fast way to assess basic skills and standards."

"If only I had a way to find out what my students already know about language!"

"If only I had a good way to find out what my students have learned!"

"How can I tell if my students are ready for state assessments?"

"It takes too long to create my own tests on the units I teach."

"The tests that come with my textbooks are too long and too dull."

"I need tests that cover all the skills on a topic—not just a few here and there."

This is what teachers tell us about their needs for testing materials. If you, too, are looking for quality, convenient materials that will help you gauge how well students are moving along towards mastering basic skills and standards—look no further. This is a book of tests such as you've never seen before! It's everything you've wanted in a group of ready-made language assessments for middle grade students.

- The tests are student-friendly. One glance through the book and you will see why. Students will be surprised that it's a test at all! The pages are inviting and fun. A wily rat and his spunky cat friend tumble over the pages, leading students through language questions and problems. Your students will not groan when you pass out these tests. They'll want to stick with them all the way to the end to see where the STOP sign is this time!

- The tests are serious. Do not be fooled by the catchy characters and visual appeal! These are serious, thorough assessments of basic content. As a part of the BASIC/Not Boring Skills Series, they give broad coverage of skills with a flair that makes them favorites of teachers and kids.

- The tests cover all the basic skill areas for language arts. There are 25 tests within 6 areas: reading, writing, grammar & usage, vocabulary & word skills, study & research skills, and spelling.

- The tests are ready to use. In convenient and manageable sizes of 4, 6, or 8 pages in length, each test covers a skill area (such as "parts of speech" or "correcting spelling errors") that should be assessed. Just give the pages to an individual student, or make copies for the entire class. Answer keys (included in back) are easy to find and easy to use.

- Skills are clearly identified. You can see exactly which skills are tested by reviewing the list of skills provided with each group of tests.

HOW TO USE THE
MIDDLE GRADE BOOK OF LANGUAGE TESTS

Each test can be used in many different ways. Here are a few:
- as a pre-test to see what a student knows or can do on a certain language topic
- as a post-test to find out how well students have mastered a content or skill area
- as a review to check up on student mastery of standards or readiness for state assessments
- as a survey to provide direction for your present or future instruction
- as an instructional tool to guide students through a review of a lesson
- with one student in an assessment or tutorial setting
- with a small group of students for assessment or instruction
- with a whole class for end-of-unit assessment

The book provides you with tools for using the tests effectively and keeping track of how students are progressing on skills or standards:

- **25 Tests on the Topics You Need:** These are grouped according to broad topics within language. Each large grouping has three or more sub-tests. Tests are clearly labeled with subject area and specific topic.

- **Skills Checklists Correlated to Test Items:** At the beginning of each group of tests, you'll find a list of the skills covered. (For instance, pages 10 and 11 hold lists of skills for the four reading tests.) Each skill is matched with the exact test items assessing that skill. If a student misses an item on the test, you'll know exactly which skill needs sharpening.

- **Student Progress Records:** Page 154 holds a reproducible form that can be used to track individual student achievement on all the tests in this book. Make a copy of this form for each student, and record the student's test scores and areas of instructional need.

- **Class Progress Records:** Pages 155–157 hold reproducible forms for keeping track of a whole class. You can record the dates that tests are given, and keep comments about what you learned from that test as well as notes for further instructional needs.

- **Reference for Skill Sharpening Activities:** Pages 158-159 describe a program of appealing exercises designed to teach, strengthen, or reinforce basic language skills and content. The skills covered in these books are correlated to national curriculum standards and the standards for many states.

- **Scoring Guide for Performance Test:** A performance test is given for writing. For a complete scoring guide that assesses student performance on this test, see pages 166–167.

- **Answer Keys:** An easy-to-use answer key is provided for each of the 25 language tests. (See pages 161–176.)

THE MIDDLE GRADE LANGUAGE TESTS

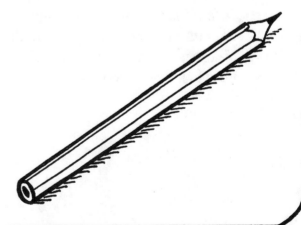

Reading Skills Checklists

Reading Test # 1:

WORD MEANINGS

Test Location: pages 12–17

Skill	*Test Items*
Determine word meaning from sentence context	1–4
Determine word meaning from paragraph context	5, 6
Determine meaning of phrases from context	7–9
Recognize and use synonyms	10–13
Recognize and use antonyms	14–17
Choose the correct word for the context of a sentence	18, 19
Use knowledge of prefixes to determine word meaning	20–25
Use knowledge of suffixes to determine word meaning	26–31
Identify the meaning of the root of a word	32–43
Identify multiple meanings of a word	44–45
Explain literal meaning of idioms	46–50

Reading Test # 2:

LITERAL COMPREHENSION

Test Location: pages 18–25

Skill	*Test Items*
Identify literal main ideas	1, 2
Read to find details and information	3–7, 9–11, 13–20
Choose the best title for a selection	8, 12, 21
Identify details that support an opinion or idea	22, 23
Determine sequence of events in a passage	24, 32
Gain information from titles, headlines, or captions	24–27
Make use of graphics to gain understanding of a text	28–31
Read to follow directions	33–40

Reading Test # 3:

INFERENTIAL & EVALUATIVE COMPREHENSION

Test Location: pages 26–33

Skill	*Test Items*
Identify implied main ideas	1, 2
Identify the intended audience for a passage	3
Recognize the author's beliefs or biases	4, 5
Recognize the author's purpose	6, 15, 21
Distinguish between fact and opinion in a passage	7–11
Identify cause-effect relationships	12–14
Draw logical conclusions from a written text	16, 20
Make generalizations based on material read	17–19
Read to interpret charts, graphs, and tables	17–19
Use information gained from a text to make predictions	22–24
Evaluate ideas, conclusions, or opinions from a text	25
Use information gained from a text to make inferences	26–30

Reading Test # 4:

LITERATURE SKILLS

Test Location: pages 34–39

Skill	*Test Items*
Identify the setting of a piece of writing	1
Identify main and supporting characters	2, 3
Identify the form of a piece of writing	4, 8–12
Identify other elements (theme, tone, mood) of a piece of writing	5, 6, 13–15
Identify and analyze characteristics of different characters	7
Identify the rhyming pattern of a poem	16
Recognize sensory appeal in a piece of writing	17
Identify literary devices and their effects (alliteration, simile, metaphor, rhyme, rhythm, repetition, puns, personification, idioms, hyperbole, quotation, imagery)	18–36
Recognize effective use of words and phrases to accomplish a purpose in the writing	37, 42
Identify the author's bias or feelings about the subject	38, 41
Recognize the audience for a piece of writing	39
Recognize the purpose of a piece of writing	40
Recognize literal meanings of figures of speech	43–47
Identify the meanings of various literary terms	48–55

Copyright ©2001 by Incentive Publications, Inc., Nashville, TN.

WORD MEANINGS

Name _____

Date _____

Possible Correct Answers: 50

Your Correct Answers: _____

Before leaving the boat, the divers **conferred** about safety during the upcoming dive.

1. Is this sentence, **conferred** means:
   a. congratulated one another.
   b. embraced.
   c. worried.
   d. compared views.

He came out of the rock fall unhurt. It is amazing that he could **extricate** himself from that rubble.

3. In this passage, **extricate** means:
   a. protect.
   b. free.
   c. bury.
   d. surround.

The judges showed high **esteem** for the rock climber's accomplishments.

2. Is this sentence, **esteem** means:
   a. jealousy.
   b. contempt.
   c. regard.
   d. worry.

I heard this snowboard competition was sold out weeks ago. How did you manage to **procure** these four tickets today?

4. Is this passage, **procure** means:
   a. give away.
   b. get possession of.
   c. sell.
   d. borrow.

12

A group of 20 bikers gathered at the base of the mountain. They were **all fired up** about the big race. Soon these tough athletes would **scale a peak** on a treacherous, **craggy** course.

We were **confounded** to see Charlie arrive at the course. Charlie spends most of his days surfing the wild waves of the California coast. We had never seen him anywhere but at the beach. In his flowered shorts and bare feet, he looked like a **fish out of water** at this race.

5. In the first paragraph, **craggy** means:
   a. tiring.
   b. long.
   c. rocky.
   d. crazy.

6. In the second paragraph, **confounded** means:
   a. disappointed.
   b. surprised.
   c. happy.
   d. troubled.

7. When the passage says the bikers **were all fired up**, it means:
   a. they would begin the race with the firing of a gun.
   b. they were very excited about the race.
   c. part of the race course would pass through fire.
   d. they were angry because the race course was so difficult.

8. When the passage says the athletes would **scale a peak**, it means:
   a. the bikers would measure the height of the mountain.
   b. the path would be smoothed out for the bikers.
   c. the mountain peak had many scaly rocks along the path.
   d. during the race, the bikers would climb a mountain.

9. When the passage says Charlie looked like a **fish out of water**, it means:
   a. Charlie looked like he did not belong in this group.
   b. Charlie was dripping wet in his bathing suit.
   c. Charlie was carrying fish.
   d. Charlie had the appearance of a fish.

Read the ad for *Extreme Sports, Inc.* In the ad, find and write a **synonym** for each of these words:

10. control _____

11. valor _____

12. explore _____

13. capture _____

Read the ad for *Extreme Sports, Inc.* In the ad, find and write an **antonym** for each of these words:

14. secure _____

15. moderate _____

16. dislike _____

17. withstand _____

hang gliding *surfing* *bungee jumping*

free fall

EXTREME SPORTS, INC.
Lessons in Radical Outdoor Enterprises

Learn to command a speeding ice yacht!

Probe the depths of the underwater world!

Take your courage and skill to the air: try hang gliding!

Relish the thrills of the biggest waves!

Succumb to the desire for a free fall!

Take a precarious walk across the high wire!

Try the pursuit of your dreams today.

ice yachting

scuba diving *high wire*

Choose the correct word for the context of each sentence.

18. Six weary skiers had _____ through deep snow into the later hours of the day.

    a. wandered   b. zigzagged   c. trudged   d. skidded

19. With great _____ they stumbled into the warm comfort of the lodge.

    a. surprise   b. relief   c. vivacity   d. regret

Name _____

Middle Grade Book of Language Tests

Copyright ©2001 by Incentive Publications, Inc., Nashville, TN.

Use your knowledge of **prefixes** to choose the correct word for each definition.

20. carry across a place a. export b. transport c. import	**22. place somewhere else** a. displace b. replace c. misplace	**24. against war** a. post-war b. anti-war c. pro-war
21. fit in a good way a. misfit b. unfit c. benefit	**23. after the game** a. pre-game b. mid-game c. post-game	**25. under water** a. submarine b. ultramarine c. marinate

Use your knowledge of **suffixes** to choose the correct word for each definition.

26. without friends a. friendliness b. friendship c. friendless	**29. person who acts** a. active b. actor c. action
27. act of being inspected a. inspection b. inspector c. inspectable	**30. in a kind manner** a. kindly b. kindness c. kinder
28. able to be eaten a. eatery b. eating c. edible	**31. like a hero** a. heroism b. heroic c. heroism

Name _____

Middle Grade Book of Language Tests

Write the **meaning of the root word** in each of these words.
Choose a meaning from the chart.

foot	32. portable _____
work	33. dormitory _____
cut	34. suspension _____
carry	35. operate _____
break	36. bisect _____
hand	37. thermometer _____
words	38. centipede _____
heat	39. fracture _____
look-see	40. tangible _____
hang	41. verbal _____
touch	42. visual _____
sleep	43. manual _____

Name _____

Middle Grade Book of Language Tests

44. Which is NOT a meaning of **seal**?

   a. a mark or emblem

   b. to fasten or secure

   c. a high-pitched sound

   d. a marine animal

   e. a tight closure

45. Which is NOT a meaning of **note**?

   a. importance

   b. to ignore

   c. a brief letter

   d. money

   e. to notice

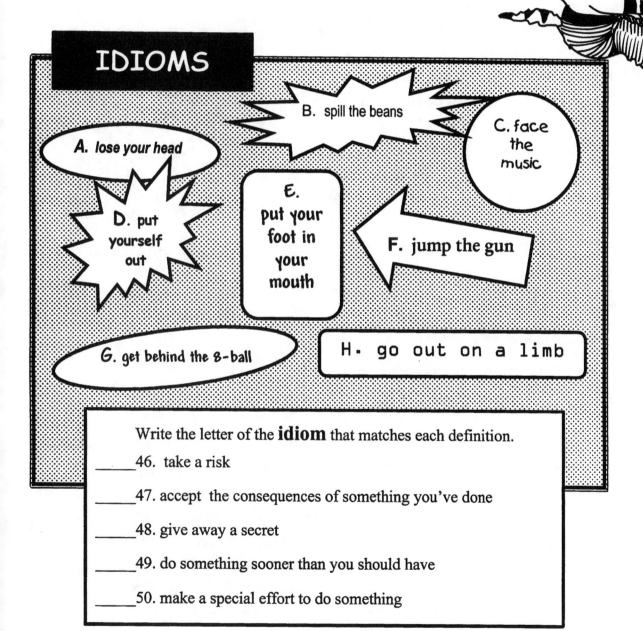

IDIOMS

A. lose your head

B. spill the beans

C. face the music

D. put yourself out

E. put your foot in your mouth

F. jump the gun

G. get behind the 8-ball

H. go out on a limb

Write the letter of the **idiom** that matches each definition.

_____46. take a risk

_____47. accept the consequences of something you've done

_____48. give away a secret

_____49. do something sooner than you should have

_____50. make a special effort to do something

Name _____

17

Middle Grade Book of Language Tests

LITERAL COMPREHENSION

Name _____

Possible Correct Answers: 40

Date _____

Your Correct Answers: _____

Read the paragraph below.

> You can imagine that walking on water is a rather tough thing to do. Yet, it seems that walking on your hands may be even harder. The world records for these events hint at this. A water-walker covered 3502 miles on skis to set the record. The person who walked on his hands, however, could cover only 870 miles.

1. What is the main idea?

   a. It is easy to walk on water.

   b. It is difficult to walk on your hands.

   c. It is probably harder to walk on hands than on water.

   d. Water-walking and hand-walking are hard.

Read this passage.

> [1]Some skiers have been frightened by the loud sound of snowboards. [2]Others have not approved of the baggy snowboarder attire. [3]The aggressive behavior of snowboarders bothers some, too. [4]All in all, snowboarders have not been welcomed on many ski hills until recently.

2. Which sentence contains the main idea? Write the number. _____

A "wall" of water: it's the big wave that surfers wait for, and thrill to ride. Thousands of surfers all over the world rush into wild surf day after day, looking for that perfect big wave. Sometimes these perfect waves are as high as 30 feet!

When they find the perfect wave, how do they ride it? The idea is to ride along the vertical face of the big wave just ahead of the wave's crest. That's the place where it is breaking. Of course, the surfer needs to stay ahead of the crest and not get crashed under it.

Surfers start by kneeling or lying on the surfboard and paddling out to the area beyond where the waves are breaking. Here they wait for the right wave. When a surfer sees a good wave coming, she turns and paddles furiously toward shore, trying to move as fast as the wave. If she times it right, the wave will pick up her surfboard and carry it along. At this point she will stand up on the board at the top of the wave and ride it down the wall or vertical face of the wave. She actually gets going faster than the wave is moving. She must keep an eye on the wave's crest and turn to the board so the board stays ahead of the crest.

If she gets it right, the surfer can enjoy a nice ride for several minutes, moving at a good speed—up to 10 miles an hour. Or, if she doesn't get it right, she can be wiped out (sent smashing beneath the water by the tremendous heavy weight and force of a monstrous wave)!

3. What is the surfer's first movement when she sees the right wave coming?
   a. stand up
   b. paddle toward the shore
   c. paddle into the wave
   d. lie down on the board

4. At what point in the process does the surfer stand up?

   _____

5. What part of the wave does the surfer ride?

   _____

6. What will happen if the surfer does not stay ahead of the crest?

   _____

7. What does the article tell about the size of surfboards?

   _____

8. Which title is best for the passage?
   a. Why Surfing is Dangerous
   b. Riding the Wall
   c. Why Surfing is a Thrill
   d. The Structure of Waves

Tattoos have been used for many purposes for hundreds of years. They have been a mark of membership in a group or a sign of rank in a group. Some tattoos were worn as protection against evil or ill fortune. Others showed courage. Tattoos were used to brand criminals, or to serve as disguises. But mostly, through history, tattoos have been used for decoration. Today, tattoos are becoming popular as a fashion item of body decoration. Since the 1980s, the tattoo process is even being used to add permanent eyeliner or lip color. With the practice on the rise, many people are considering getting a tattoo.

What, exactly, is a tattoo? It is a permanent design decorating the human body. Tattoos are made by cutting or pricking the skin and inserting a colored dye or pigment under the skin. The modern tattoo process uses electric needles. In the past, instruments such as knives, thorns, and sharpened bones were used.

Is it a good idea to slice your skin and put color under it permanently? Many doctors don't think so. Serious side effects often accompany tattoos. Besides plaguing infections and eye damage from the permanent eyeliner, cancers have been linked to tattoos. Contaminated needles and equipment can also spread diseases, including AIDS. Many parents are irate that a child can get a tattoo without their permission. A parent's signature is required for ear piercing for minors in most states—yet kids can often get tattoos without parental permission. One of the major concerns about tattooing is that there are few controls or restrictions on the process. No training or licensing is required in many places. As a customer seeking a tattoo, you cannot be sure of the person's ability, experience, carefulness, or of the safety or cleanliness of their equipment.

So think about this: **when you get a tattoo, what else are you getting?**

9. Which is NOT one of the reasons mentioned for tattoos?

    a. decoration   b. disguise   c. to frighten enemies   d. membership in a group   e. protection

10. What is mentioned as a recent use of tattooing?_____

11. Whish is NOT mentioned as a danger of tattooing?

    a. disease spread   b. infections   c. itching and soreness   d. cancer

12. Which title best fits the passage?

    a. The History of Tattooing   b. How to Tattoo   c. To Tattoo or Not to Tattoo?

Name _____

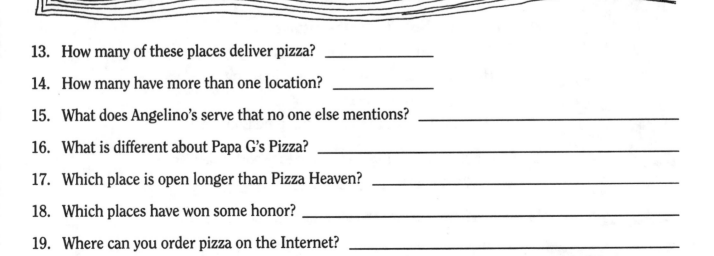

ANGELINO'S PIZZA

Authentic Chicago Style Pizza

Roasted Chicken, Calzone, Pasta

Televised Sports Every Day

OPEN 11 A.M.-1 A.M. 7 days a week

6666 Beltway   Phone 668-9222

Free Delivery

Order Online: www.angelino.com

PIZZA HEAVEN

Pizza • Pasta • Salad Bar

4 Locations

22 W. Main	772-1919
3000 Cascade	775-0001
151 Black Oak	772-1000
Pete's Plaza	776-9292

Voted Best Pizza in Town, 1999

Open 7 Days noon-midnight

Chicago Style Deep-Dish Pizza

40 Varieties of Pizza

Take Out—Delivery—Dine In

800 Highway 44

447-9081

BRUNO'S PIZZA

PAPA G'S PIZZARIA

Award-Winning Pizza

You Bake at Home

11:00 A.M. – 11 P.M. Daily

West Side Plaza   662-2098

90 N. Broadway   664-8888

13. How many of these places deliver pizza? _____

14. How many have more than one location? _____

15. What does Angelino's serve that no one else mentions? _____

16. What is different about Papa G's Pizza? _____

17. Which place is open longer than Pizza Heaven? _____

18. Which places have won some honor? _____

19. Where can you order pizza on the Internet? _____

20. What information does the ad give about Bruno's hours? _____

Name _____   **21**   _____

1 The first bungee jumpers were called land divers. They jumped from trees, towers, or cliffs with vines tied to their legs.

2 Early U.S. bungee jumpers mostly jumped from bridges. Now, they also jump from platforms, cliffs, helicopters, balloons, and other high places. Great attention came to bungee jumping in 1987 when someone jumped from the Eiffel Tower.

3 There have been injuries and deaths in the sport. Most of these were caused by the jumper's error or lack of safety precautions.

4 Bungee jumping combines the thrill and danger of free fall with the assurance that the cord will save you from disaster.

5 Bungee jumping is a relatively safe sport for beginners.

6 There are two systems for bungee jumping, The New Zealand system uses one cord whose length depends on the weight of the jumper. The U.S. system uses one cord for each 50 pounds of weight, and jumpers wear two harnesses.

7 Statistically, there is a greater chance of being injured or killed in a car than of being injured or killed while bungee jumping.

8 Some inventive bungee jumpers ride bikes, kayaks, unicycles, trash cans, skateboards, or motorcycles as they jump.

9 There are reports of injuries to eyes and limbs caused by the shock of the abrupt stop at the end of the bungee cord.

10 When all safety procedures are followed, the bungee jump stops a fall just as safely as the brakes stop a car traveling down hill.

21. Which is the best title for the passage?
    a. Things to Know about Bungee Jumping
    b. How to Master the Art of Bungee Jumping
    c. The History of Bungee Jumping
    d. Beginner's Guide to Bungee Jumping Equipment

22. Which items support the idea that the sport is dangerous?
    Write the numbers. _____

23. Which items support the idea that the sport is safe?
    Write the numbers. _____

Name _____

Middle Grade Book of Language Tests

The Gazette, September 4, 1995

FRENCHMAN FREE DIVES 240 FEET TO SET RECORD

Morning News, March 6, 1983

High Speed Water Ski Record Broken Yesterday

Daily Tidings, Saturday, July 22, 2000

BOOMERANG CONTEST BEGINS NEXT THURSDAY

The Tribune, December 10, 1979

MAN EATS RECORD 19 BANANAS IN 2 MINUTES

The Evening News, February 10, 1992

YODELING SPEED RECORD BROKEN YESTERDAY

The City Gazette, July 24, 2000

Local Girl Wins Torch-Juggling Contest Today

24. Number these events in the order that they happened.

_____ water ski record broken

_____ banana-eating record set

_____ torch-juggling contest

_____ free dive record set

_____ yodeling speed record broken

_____ beginning of boomerang contest

25. What date was the yodeling record broken? _____

26. What date did the boomerang contest begin? _____

27. Which event happened before the water ski record? _____

Name _____ **23** _____

STRANGE & AMAZING JOURNEYS

996 miles in 245 hours

3100 miles in 107 days

3008 miles in 107 days

3261 miles in 44 days

870 miles in 55 days

3366 miles in 42 days

28. Which trip covered more miles than the unicycle trip?

   a. lawnmower b. backwards run c. stilts

29. How much longer (in days) was the backwards runner's journey than the hand sprinter's? _____

30. Which trip was about 34 days longer than the leapfrog journey?

   a. lawnmower b. hand spring c. unicycle

31. About how many miles shorter was the stilts trip than the backwards run?

   a. 300   b. 100   c. 200

32. This limerick is out of order.
    Number the lines 1–5 in the correct sequence.

   ____ To the east coast in 42 days.

   ____ He took his lawn mower from the west

   ____ Well, he had ten thousand dollars to raise.

   ____ And rode it all across the U.S.

   ____ Why's this 12-year-old getting great praise?

Middle Grade Book of Language Tests

33. Give the contestant next to #14 a 3-digit number > 116.

34. Give the contestant next to #16 a 2-digit number with no digits < 5.

35. Draw glasses on the contestant with the lowest number.

36. Draw the grape which contestant #14 has just spit.

37. Show contestant #16 spitting a cricket.

38. Draw a hat on the contestant with the highest number.

39. Draw the grape that was spit by the contestant with glasses.

40. Draw the final contestant spitting a watermelon seed.

Name _____

INFERENTIAL & EVALUATIVE COMPREHENSION

Name _____   Possible Correct Answers: 30

Date _____   Your Correct Answers: _____

Most records are set with active feats
Of speed or strength or skill.
But did you know that prizes go
To folks who just are still?

Some dive from planes or walk on ropes.
Some juggle two-edged swords.
To win renown, some wrestle snakes
Or surf through the air on boards.

But records, too, are broken
For doing nothing at all.
For standing still, sitting in trees,
Or relaxing on a wall.

1. The main idea of the poem is:

    a. Most records are set with a strenuous activity.

    b. Active records are more impressive than inactive ones.

    c. Records can be set for something that requires no activity.

    d. Someone has set a record for standing still.

When you explore a cave, you may not be aware that your presence is harmful to the cave. Many caves have been destroyed by pollution, litter, or damage left by those who visit them. Take care not to mar or break any structures of the cave. When you finish enjoying the natural beauties of the underground world, leave nothing behind. Be aware that even the slightest impact or smallest amount of litter can bring harm to the cave.

2. The main idea of the passage is:

    a. Caves are being destroyed.

    b. Cave visitors should treat caves with care.

    c. Caves are full of litter.

3. This passage was probably written for:

    a. people who read about caves.

    b. school children learning about caves.

    c. people who explore caves.

Middle Grade Book of Language Tests   Copyright ©2001 by Incentive Publications, Inc., Nashville, TN.

Dear Leroy,

Congratulations on your graduation! I hear you plan to celebrate with a big adventure—learning to sky dive. I'm sure that is a most interesting sport. I wonder what made you decide to choose that activity. Did your schooling teach you to be so foolishly brave that you would think it is safe for you?

Don't you remember how clumsy you were with your scuba diving equipment? Have you forgotten your near-fatal hang gliding accident? Are you overlooking your history of close calls and serious mistakes with extreme sports?

Well, have fun with your adventure. I do hope I see you again.

Your faithful Aunt Rita

4. The author of the letter probably believes:
   a. Sky diving is an exciting adventure for her nephew.
   b. Sky diving is too dangerous for her nephew.
   c. Her nephew will do a fine job of sky diving.
   d. Leroy should be scuba diving or hang gliding instead.

5. The author tells her nephew to have fun with his adventure. Most likely, what is her real attitude as she says this?
   a. She really wants him to have fun sky diving.
   b. She is angry at his poor schooling.
   c. She is terribly worried that he will get hurt.

6. Aunt Rita's main purpose in writing this letter was probably:
   a. to subtly convince him to change his mind about sky diving.
   b. to state very clearly that she did not approve of his sky diving.
   c. to show how interested she is in sky diving.

Name _____

Label each of these sentences from the passage as F (fact) or O (opinion).

Interview with an ACW Climber

Interviewer: What in the world is an ACW, anyway?

Climber: It's the key feature in a great new sport. ACW is an artificial climbing wall.

Interviewer: Describe these ACWs.

Climber: These walls are not the rocks climbed in natural outdoor settings. They are created artificially with materials other than rock. Usually the ACW is used indoors.

Interviewer: Why climb an ACW instead of a real rock?

Climber: They are easy to get to without long hikes. The climber doesn't have to worry about weather. Climbers can learn or practice climbing skills in a safer setting that is not extremely high.

Interviewer: Which is more appealing to climbers: real rocks or an ACW?

Climber: Everybody is happier climbing an ACW because it is safer.

Interviewer: I hear this is a fast-growing activity. Why?

Climber: Everyone should do this. ACW climbing is safer and more accessible to beginners. Because of that, more people are learning to climb.

_____ 7. Everyone should do this.

_____ 8. ACW is an artificial climbing wall.

_____ 9. They are created artificially with materials other than rock.

_____10. Everybody is happier climbing an ACW.

_____11. The climber doesn't have to worry about weather.

12. The accessibility and safety of ACW climbing (cause) leads to an effect described in the passage. Write a sentence that describes that effect.

_____

_____

_____

_____

_____

13. In this pair of sentences, one sentence tells a cause. The other tells the effect.
Circle the letter of the sentence that describes an **effect**.

   a. A ski jumper starts down the hill in a crouched position.

   b. This position cuts down on wind resistance and allows the skier to pick up speed.

14. In this group of sentences, one sentence tells a cause. Another tells an effect.
Circle the letter of the sentence that describes a **cause** of something.

   a. Snowboarders enjoyed the thrill of getting down the hill.

   b. Once they got down, they wanted a way to get back up.

   c. So they added sails to their boards and sailed back up the hill.

Could You Be a Record-Setter?

If you want to set or break a record for the *Guinness Book of Records*, start thinking about what you can do. Read all the current records. Decide if you will try to break one of those or create a new activity. Write to the Guinness Records address to apply for a new activity or get guidelines. You'll need to learn all the guidelines for your challenge. It is important to keep careful records of your record attempts. Two reliable persons or organizations must witness all records. Each record attempt must also be recorded on videotape.

15. The author of this passage probably wrote this to:

   a. brag about his records.

   b. give people ideas about kinds of records they could set.

   c. give some information about the record-setting process.

16. From the information given in the passage, you can conclude that:

   a. If you want to set a record, you need to create a new activity.

   b. It is relatively easy to set a new record.

   c. It takes time and planning to set a record.

   d. Thousands of people try to set records.

GUIDED ADVENTURE TRIPS

Trip	Time	Trip Cost	Equipment Rental Cost	Insurance Cost per day
WATER SPORTS				
Scuba Diving	8 am-2 pm	$95	$100	$14
Windsurfing	10 am-noon	$75	$75	$5
Snorkeling	noon-5 pm	$30	$20	$5
AIR SPORTS				
Hang Gliding	8 am-4 pm	$200	$150	$20
Sky Surfing 5-day trip	Mon-Fri 8 am-5 pm	$750	$250	$45
Skydiving 3-day trip	Mon-Wed 9 am-4 pm	$400	$185	$45
LAND SPORTS				
Land Yachting	9 am-1 pm	$60	$75	$4
Street Luge	noon-5 pm	$55	$50	$7
Rock Climbing	7 am-7 pm	$80	$70	$10

17. Can you say that the air adventures involve all-day trips? _____

18. Which generalization can be made from the information given on the table of trip information?

    a. For most trips, equipment rental nearly doubles the cost of the trip.

    b. Insurance is a major part of the cost for all the trips.

    c. The water sports are the safest of all the trips.

    d. The longest trips are the water trips.

19. Which generalization can NOT be made from the information given on the table?

    a. The air sports are generally the most expensive.

    b. The air sports are the most dangerous.

    c. All of the shortest trips are land adventures.

TEACHER'S FIELD TRIP BLUES

I am never taking this class on a field trip again! I mean it! Never!

The trouble started, as it always does, with the bus ride to the marine park. Jason somehow sneaked a salami sandwich on the bus, even though I had collected all the lunches into my care before we boarded the bus. Very soon, the sandwich ended up under Rosa Benson. By the time we left the school parking lot, the mustard was all over her white shorts, the bus seat, Ramon's new jacket, and Jennifer's hair. And it was only minutes later that Melanie sprayed hairspray on the bus driver and Louis threw up his breakfast.

I won't even try to describe the noise level on the bus, or the other bus disasters. I will only mention that fish in one marine tank are now enjoying chocolate milk, twenty-six 5th graders have wet clothes, the $50 bill that Kim's mother let her bring is in the belly of a large shark, two of my students thought they could ride the killer whale, and the aquarium manager requested we refrain from a visit next year.

And while I'm complaining, I will express my annoyance at the way the parent chaperones manage to avoid having any impact on the chaos. Mrs. Vincent spent most of her time in the bathroom doing her makeup and hair after getting drenched in the dolphin show. Mr. Hornsby said something like this every three minutes: "My children aren't allowed to be this disrespectful." (His children were spraying drinking fountain water down the collars of the kindergartners from St. Mary's School.) Mrs. Flannery kept wringing her hands and saying, "Can't you DO something with them?"

"No I can't!" I said to myself. "But what I can do," I said—also to myself, "is never, ever, set foot in an aquarium, zoo, planetarium, museum, or marine park with anyone under 25—ever again!"

20. From reading this passage, what can you conclude?

   a. The parent chaperones were very helpful.

   b. Several students got hurt.

   c. The adults had little control over the students.

21. The author probably wrote this to:

   a. tell the value of field trips.

   b. let off steam.

   c. complain about the marine park services.

22. Which of these is most likely to happen?

   a. The teacher will quit teaching.

   b. This teacher will plan field trips more carefully in the future.

   c. The teacher will go teach college.

Name

31

For a whole year, Spike had looked forward to his trip to the amusement park on the west coast near his grandparents' home. The main attraction was the colossal new roller coaster, *Goliath.* Spike has ridden 84 different coasters. This new one would be the steepest drop of his coaster-riding career.

He got to the park early. Much to his disappointment, the line for *Goliath* had a 3-hour wait. If he waited for the 3 hours, he knew he would miss out on using his ticket for other rides. But the line for *Goliath* would probably get longer as the day went along.

23. What will Spike probably do next?

   a. Go home.

   b. Stay in the line for *Goliath.*

   c. Go home.

   d. Forget *Goliath* and ride other coasters.

The third skater hit a huge crack in the path. She tumbled head over heels, smashing her knee into a tree. There was an obvious gash. She dragged herself back near the path so other skaters could see her. She waited, her head spinning. Her vision began to get fuzzy.

24. What is most likely to happen next?

   a. She'll resume the race right away.

   b. She'll resume the race later.

   c. Another skater will see her and send for help.

20 bikers started the race. 15 were over 16 years old. 16 of the 20 wore black and red biking tights. 7 of the bikers were from the *Lost Valley Bike Team.* 10 bikers wore silver helmets.

The top 5 finishers were under 16. All of these winning bikers had silver helmets. 4 of the top 5 were members of the *Lost Valley Bike Team.*

Leroy watched the race. He concluded that:

1) The black & red tights made riders faster.
2) The silver helmets brought good luck .
3) The younger bikers were strong riders.
4) The *Lost Valley Team* had trained well.

25. Read Leroy's conclusions. Which ones are reasonable?

   Write the numbers: _____

Name _____

Middle Grade Book of Language Tests

THE CASE OF THE SABOTAGED LOCKERS

The mascot of the North High School Rams, a small ram named Rambo, disappeared during the second half of the homecoming game. Frantic fans and school officials searched the football field, stands, concession booths, parking lot, and locker rooms for hours. They found nothing. But on Monday morning, inside the school, some clues began to turn up.

Five students, whose lockers were in a row, could not get their lockers open. Furthermore, some strange sounds, smells, and liquids were emanating from the lockers. School administrators stomped around authoritatively, gruffly questioning students—particularly the owners of these lockers: Matt, Michelle, Andrea, Scott, and Tara. Custodians, wearing an official air, bustled around with tools for cracking open the lockers. This is what the investigation revealed:

- One strange item was found in each of the 5 lockers.
- Locker #119 contained a frightened, messy, squeaking rat.
- The ram was not in locker #117.
- Matt's locker is between Michelle's and Andrea's.
- Tara's locker has the lowest number.
- The locker next to Andrea's held a large garlic pizza.
- Locker #118 did not have any food in it.
- Ten melting snowballs were found in Scott's locker.
- Andrea's locker is next to Tara's.
- The locker hiding the ram was next to a locker with a huge bag of Chinese food.
- The owner of the locker between the Chinese food and the rat is the culprit who had kidnapped Rambo.

26. From the passage, what would you infer was the mood of the school officials?

    a. amused   b. casual   c. serious   d. furious

27. Which locker is Scott's? _____

28. Which locker held the pizza? _____

29. Which locker held the ram? _____

30. Who kidnapped the ram? _____

Middle Grade Book of Language Tests

LITERATURE SKILLS

Name _____   Possible Correct Answers: 55

Date _____   Your Correct Answers: _____

> My sister, Latitia, is the most entertaining person I know. Every weekend and summer day, she turns our backyard into a regular theater of excitement. She has made a habit of trying out weird and wacky antics. Every one seems more unique and wild than the last.
>
> One weekend, she'll be balancing glasses on her chin. The next, she'll be making a sandwich that reaches around the whole yard. She has eaten record numbers of pickled eggs, raced pet mice inside roller-skates up and down the driveway, climbed ladders upside down while holding a flaming torch in her teeth, built a scarecrow taller than our house, and invited the whole town to a paper clip chain-making party.
>
> Often she will involve all the neighborhood kids in the fun. They have joined her for bathtub races, backward lawn-mower pushing, cricket-spitting contests, bubble-blowing competitions, and sausage-eating marathons. Last weekend, her whole soccer team was here to balance eggs on spoons. Next week, her eighth grade class is coming for an onion-peeling race.
>
> There is never a dull moment living with Latitia!

1. The **setting** of the story is _____   2. Who is the **main character**? _____

3. Name the **supporting characters**._____

4. This passage is a: a. poem   b. parable   c. news report   d. story   e. myth

5. The author's **tone** in this passage is: a. annoyed   b. resentful   c. admiring   d. haughty

6. The **mood** of the passage is: a. solemn   b. joyful   c. silly   d. eerie

7. From this passage you can tell that Latitia is (*circle one or more*):

   a. creative   b. troublesome   c. moody   d. adventuresome   e. unusual

Each selection below (8-12) is taken from a different form of literature.
Write one of these labels on each selection:

| letter | essay | poem | parable | news report |
| joke | biography | interview | myth | advertisement |

8

Dozens of people have hobbies they love.
They cook, sew a quilt, design cakes.
But no one I've known or have heard of
Has a hobby as wacky as Jake's.

He doesn't collect stamps or rare posters.
He doesn't paint pictures of lakes.
Instead, he sits for hours in a bathtub,
Surrounded by poisonous snakes.

9

Ed: What do you call the towel that a snake uses after his bath?
Fred: A viper wiper.

10

Jake Abernathy grew up on the streets of Philadelphia. At age 3, while on a camping trip, he saw his first snake. Ever since then, he has spent every spare minute with snakes. By age 10, he could cite facts about thousands of snake varieties. His interest in snakes led him to the hobby of snake-sitting. In the past 5 years, he has won 29 major snake-sitting titles, making him the number one snake-sitter in the state and region.

11

SNAKE-SITTER SETS RECORD

Twenty competitors from 12 counties took part in a snake-sitting competition that was held in Lane City last week. Jake Abernathy, a local favorite, took home the top honors. He sat in a bathtub for several hours over the week-long period with 29 rattlesnakes. This is Jake's 28th win in this unusual activity. The prize for second place went to 25-year old Sarabeth Samson, who sat with 22 snakes.

12

LEARN THE ART OF SNAKE-SITTING
You too can safely sit in a tub with a dozen rattlesnakes.
No bites! No danger!
Lessons by Jake
State Champion Snake-Sitter
Call 508-9999
or email: www.jakesnake@viper.com

Name _____

35

A

I'd sooner romance a gorilla
Or go to a dance with Godzilla,
I'd sooner agree to be King Kong's mate,
Than find stewed tomatoes on my plate.

B.

You need to have a stomach strong
To eat my sister's cooking,
Or else, bring a dog along,
To feed it to when she's not looking.

C.

Don't expect me to eat oysters
Because the taste I could not stand
I'd rather swallow goldfish live
Or chew a bag of sand.

I'd eat my Walkman, eat the tapes,
Chew the earphones any day.
But put an oyster on my tongue—
Are you kidding? No, no way!

You can torture me with scorpions,
Hang snakes from all my walls,
Fill my bathtub with piranhas,
Push me over Niagara Falls.

You can swear to light my underwear,
Dunk me in boiling water to my hips.
No matter what you threaten,
Oysters will never touch these lips.

13. What is the theme of the poems? _____

14. The tone of Poems A, B, and C is

   a. angry   b. serious

   c. humorous   d. judgmental

15. The tone of Poem D is

   a. silly   b. negative

   c. sympathetic d. angry

16. Circle the rhyming pattern of poem A

   a, b, a, b   a, a, b, b   a, b, c, b

17. Poem D mainly appeals to the sense of

   a. sight   b. sound   c. smell   d. taste

18. Find a line in one of the poems that is an example
    of alliteration. Circle that line.

D.

Have you ever really looked at a sausage?
A slick brown sausage, a hot blunt stinky sausage
With little pieces of grainy fat stuck in on the sides?
A slinky slippery slimy serpentine sausage?
A gushy fuzzy with mold reeking sausage?
A wrinkly crinkly scabby sausage?
Have you ever really looked at a sausage?

Name _____

36

The lines and sentences below use the literary devices shown on Spike's list.
Identify at least one device used for each example. Write the code letter on the line.

_____19. Rat-a-tat-tat, what noise is that?

_____20. *I'm going out on a limb to do this for you.*

_____21. **Her smile is as genuine as counterfeit dollar.**

_____22. *Visiting the dentist is a fulfilling experience.*

_____23. It was so hot that the cows gave steamed milk.

_____24. She jumped the gun when she called for the doctor.

_____25. **Bring me some great gobs of green grease!**

_____26. *Is Dr. C. D. Stitches the new surgeon in town?*

_____27. A creaky old train grumbled about the load he had to carry.

_____28. Never again, never again will you get away with that.

_____29. **His whiny voice was a squealing siren, piercing the silence.**

_____30. **Today the fog is a grey grandfather wrapping soft arms around me.**

_____31. Is that the music calling out to me, inviting me to dance?

_____32. Which whistler was whisked away by the whooshing wind?

_____33. **The wrinkles in his face are deep as mountain crevasses.**

_____34. *A clever character named Jake makes friends each day with a rattlesnake.*

_____35. "And that's the last I want to see of you!" shouted the cheese to the mouse.

_____36. Though my math book cried out to be opened, I closed my ears.

A = alliteration
H = hyperbole
I = idiom
M = metaphor
O = onomatopoeia
P = personification
PN = pun
Q = quotation
R = rhyme
RTH = rhythm
RP = repetition
S = simile

Name _____

ODE TO SEPTEMBER

I've dreaded your arrival,
Looked forward to you, too.
Oh, month of new beginnings,
I'm glad, yet scared, of you.

I hate the loss of summer
I love the things in store.
The year'll bring mixed blessings:
Hard tests and fun galore.

New classes, new teachers,
New chances, new shoes,
Old worries, old habits,
Old friends with new news.

You bring each one back.
I'm nervous you're here
And excited, September,
You start the school year.

37. The writer uses many words and phrases to show her mixed feelings about September. Write three different pairs of words or phrases (from the poem) that show this contrast or mixture of feelings.

_____

_____

_____

38. Most likely, this writer is
    a. a student
    b. a parent
    c. a teacher

HEY SNOW BOARDERS!

Two new shops have opened. They both sell stuff for boarders. They both have great sales going on right now! *TAKE IT TO EXTREMES* is downtown. *FLIPS & TURNS* is in the mall.

Both shops have all the latest hot clothing and equipment. *TAKE IT TO EXTREMES* has the coolest salespersons. You'll love the awesome free stickers and posters they give out, too. For just $5, you can get an extremely wild T-shirt with any purchase. They cater to kids, so you feel real important as a customer. Their hours are 9 am to 9 pm, seven days a week. *FLIPS & TURNS* is open every day from noon to 10 p.m.

Get a jump on winter. Shop now for your boarding supplies!

39. This is probably intended for:
    a. snowboarders of all ages
    b. young snowboarders
    c. parents

40. This was probably written to:
    a. interest people in snowboarding
    b. advertise the businesses
    c. give information about snowboarding equipment

41. This writer seems to:
    a. feel equally positive about both shops
    b. prefer *TAKE IT TO EXTREMES*
    c. prefer *FLIPS & TURNS*

42. Write 2 words or phrases the writer uses to persuade readers to follow his advice.

_____

_____

Name _____

Write the figure of speech from the story that matches each of these meanings.

OFF HER ROCKER

Mom has lost her marbles! By 10 o'clock this morning, she had blown her top several times. When the baby dumped his cereal on his head, she lost her cool. When Jenny put the cat in the washing machine, she was fit to be tied. And when Tommy ate her lipstick, she just screamed her head off.

I think it was the toilet paper fort in the living room that was the last straw. She ran around the room yelling about how we were driving her up the wall. She just went totally bananas. After that, she just wandered around the house in a fog. I tried to keep a lid on the little kids and keep them out of her hair.

When Dad got home, he was out in the cold about her bad day. So when he shouted, "Happy birthday dear, how does it feel to be over the hill," he did not understand why she crowned him with the frying pan.

irony *contrast* *mood* *resolution* *theme* *satire* *symbols* *tone* *plot* *climax* **FLASHBACK** *contrast* *point of view* *conflict* *setting*

43. hit him on the head

_____

44. to keep control of

_____

45. making her really mad

_____

46. didn't know what was going on

_____

47. is acting really strange

_____

Write a literary term to match each description below.

_____48. the general feelings of a passage

_____49. the writer's attitude

_____50. the central idea of the passage

_____51. a jump from the present to the past in a story

_____52. the time and place of a story

_____53. the problem in a story

_____54. series of events in a story

_____55. the high point of a story

Name _____

Middle Grade Book of Language Tests

Writing Skills Checklists

Writing Test # 1:

WORD CHOICE & WORD USE

Test Location: pages 42–45

Skill	*Test Items*
Recognize and choose precise words for accurate meaning and interest	1–3
Recognize and choose effective words for strengthening written pieces	4, 5
Recognize and choose active rather than inactive words and phrases	6, 7
Identify words that help to create certain moods	8, 9
Identify sentences which have words arranged in a manner that makes meaning clear	10–13
Identify words or phrases that are repetitive or unnecessary in a written passage	14–17
Identify words or phrases that suggest the author's bias	18, 19
Recognize and choose words and phrases that produce strong sensory images; identify the sense to which the writing appeals	20–25

Writing Test # 2:

FORMS & TECHNIQUES

Test Location: pages 46–51

Skill	*Test Items*
Identify examples and uses of expository, descriptive, narrative, persuasive, and imaginative writing	1–5
Identify prose	6
Identify definitions or characteristics of different forms of writing	7–13
Identify use of writing techniques and literary devices (puns, similes, metaphors, idioms, alliteration, personification, hyperbole, onomatopoeia)	14–21, 26
Recognize the use of varied sentence structure and sentence length in a passage	22
Identify good use of details to support and enhance an idea	23
Identify the point of view from which a passage was written	24
Recognize writing where form, style, or content appeals to a specific audience	25, 35
Identify specific uses of literary techniques in a passage	26–32
Identify ways a writer uses words for a particular purpose	27, 28
Recognize sensory appeal in a passage	29, 31
Recognize writing where form, style, or content fits a certain purpose for the writing	33, 34

Writing Test # 3:

CONTENT & ORGANIZATION

Test Location: pages 52–57

Skill	*Writing Tasks*
Choose and use effective words in writing tasks	Task # 1
Create sentences that are clear and interesting	Task # 2
Create sentences that have interesting sounds and rhythms	Task # 3
Write sentences of varied structure and length	Task # 4
Create strong titles for written pieces	Task # 5
Create strong, attention-getting beginnings	Task # 6
Create strong, effective endings or conclusions	Task # 7
Include a clear main idea in a written passage	Task # 8
Show completeness and clear organization in a written piece	Task # 9
Use relevant details and examples to support a main idea	Task # 10

Writing Test # 4:

EDITING

Test Location: pages 58–63

Skill	*Editing Tasks*
Recognize and replace overused, ordinary, or inactive words and phrases	Task # 1
Revise sentences for clarity	Task # 2
Arrange ideas or lines in proper sequence	Task # 3
Eliminate excess or repetitive words or ideas in sentences	Task # 4
Eliminate repetitive unrelated ideas in passages	Task # 5
Improve weak beginnings	Task # 6
Improve weak endings or conclusions	Task # 7
Replace weak or imprecise titles	Task # 8
Strengthen a passage by adding dialogue or changing existing text to dialogue	Task # 9
Revise writing for accuracy in punctuation, capitalization, and other conventions	Task # 10

Writing Test # 5

WRITING PROCESS

Test Location: pages 64–71

Skill	*Writing Task*
The writing process test is a test of writing performance. A scoring guide (pages 166–167) is used to enable the adult to give student writers a score of 1–5 in the areas of Content, Word Choice, Sentences, Organization, Voice, and Conventions.	Entire Test

WORD CHOICE & WORD USE

Name _____

Possible Correct Answers: 25

Date _____

Your Correct Answers: _____

Choose the most **precise** word for each.

1. Her friends were _____ by Abby's terrifying tale of falling into the crevasse.
   - a. provoked
   - c. annoyed
   - b. captivated
   - d. inspired

2. "Not on your life!" _____ Mother when we told her we were planning to pierce the cat's ears.
   - a. shrieked
   - c. muttered
   - b. explained
   - d. informed

3. With cheeks full of crumbs from our pantry, the _____ mouse scuttled behind the stove.
   - a. stout
   - c. plump
   - b. burly
   - d. portly

Choose the word that is most **effective** or **interesting** for each.

4. After she discovered the band uniforms flying from the flagpole, the principle gave the students a harsh _____.
   - a. oration
   - c. admonishment
   - b. talk
   - d. response

5. The jewel thief was caught holding a most _____ necklace in his gloved hand.
   - a. pretty
   - c. fine
   - b. beautiful
   - d. exquisite

6. Which example has the most active voice?
   - a. Her heart was broken.
   - b. She had a broken heart.
   - c. Her boyfriend broke her heart.

7. Circle examples with an **active** verb.
   - a. Have you been there all along?
   - b. Never again will I do that!
   - c. Red juice splattered on her shirt.
   - d. It's apparent that the ship is gone.
   - e. "Stop," he shouted, "that's poison!"
   - f. My foot is in the shark's mouth.
   - g. Who dropped the box of eggs?
   - h. The alligator snatched my lunch.

Middle Grade Book of Language Tests

Copyright ©2001 by Incentive Publications, Inc., Nashville, TN.

8. Write a word or phrase to describe the **mood** these words would help to set._____

ill-tempered　　　*shadowy scowl*　　**SULLEN**

low grumbling　　peeve　　sulking　　discontent

9. Write a word or phrase to describe the **mood** these words would help to set._____

drowsy　　**languid**　　*sluggish steps*　　snail's pace

meandering movements　　**lethargic**

10. Which sentence is written most clearly?

a. While writing in my diary, a raccoon lept up into my window.

b. A raccoon lept into my window while I was writing in my diary.

c. A raccoon lept into my window while writing in my diary.

11. Which sentence is written most clearly?

a. Rowing across the lake a storm came up suddenly.

b. A storm came up suddenly rowing across the lake.

c. While I was rowing across the lake, a storm came up suddenly.

12. Which sentence is written most clearly?

a. After the prank, students were scolded by the principal.

b. After the prank by the principal students were scolded.

c. Students were scolded after the prank by the principal.

13. Which sentence is written most clearly?

a. After the speech, biscuits were served to the group with gravy.

b. Biscuits were served to the group after the speech with gravy.

c. After the speech, the group was served biscuits with gravy.

Name _____ 43 _____

Cross out any **unnecessary words** or **ideas** used in these sentences.

14.

This old man who was kind of like my grandfather went skydiving together with my brother.

15.

"Waitress," called the sassy customer, "what is today's soup of the day?"

16.

In my opinion, I think she has too many tattoos and also too many nose rings as well.

17.

Those two fearful 15-year-old teenagers were afraid of the stray alligators.

Look for words or phrases in these sentences that give hints of the **author's bias** about the subject. Circle those words or phrases.

18.

There are different ways to get a new musical tune. Music lovers can rush to the music store to stock up on their favorite CDs. They can buy music right from home on-line. But some deviously choose to get their favorite tunes illegally by downloading them from the Internet.

19.

I know why this rock music is really popular. It makes your pulse race with excitement and tells your happy feet to move. The clever rhymes and fetching rhythms grab the listener's ear.

Name

Middle Grade Book of Language Tests

Copyright ©2001 by Incentive Publications, Inc., Nashville, TN.

Writers use words to appeal to the different senses.

20. Which sentence evokes a strong **visual image**?
    a. Traffic lights make me wildly impatient.
    b. The traffic light winked its yellow eye at me.
    c. This is the longest traffic light in the city.

21. Which sentence appeals mostly to the sense of **touch**?
    a. Lucky lilac bush to spread its toes in the warm, soft mud.
    b. The lilac bush is surrounded by mud.
    c. We slopped and sloshed through mud to the lilac bush.

22. Which sentence evokes a **visual image**?
    a. The misty dark corner of the attic beckoned me to come explore.
    b. Faint, pained moans came from the direction of the attic.
    c. One breath of the attic air started me coughing for hours.

23. Which sentence appeals mostly to the **sense of hearing**?
    a. Where did you get that battered old jalopy?
    b. The mold and musty dust tell me that thing is a hundred years old.
    c. The motor coughed and choked, then died with a sputter and a hiss.

24. Which sentence appeals mostly to the **sense of taste**?
    a. Your gum-chewing sounds like cows walking through mud.
    b. The gum's sugar-gel center coated my mouth with grape heaven.
    c. Isn't that the largest, most purple bubble you ever saw?

25. Which sentence appeals mostly to the **sense of smell**?
    a. Hissing and squealing, the popcorn maker calls me to the kitchen.
    b. That is the largest mound of yellow kernels you've ever sold me.
    c. Waves of warm toasty corn air caressed my nose.

Name

45

FORMS & TECHNIQUES

Name _____

Possible Correct Answers: 35

Date _____

Your Correct Answers: _____

Get a good look at Spike's reading list.
Then answer the questions by writing the letter (or letters) of the pieces of writing described below.

THINGS I'VE READ THIS WEEK

A. a recipe for coffee-banana cheesecake

B. a diary entry describing events and feelings

C. a poster suggesting everyone try tuna-artichoke ice cream

D. an essay explaining someone's opinion about body piercing

E. a science fiction story about a 25th century high school

F. a letter from cousin Mike trying to convince me to visit him

G. a tall tale about a girl who could lift elephants

H. a news article about a big forest fire

I. an encyclopedia entry explaining black holes

J. a true story by Leroy about his most embarrassing moment

K. directions for getting to the airport

Write one or more letters.

1. Which are probably examples of **expository** writing? _____

2. Which are probably examples of **narrative** writing? _____

3. Which are probably examples of **persuasive** writing? _____

4. Which are probably examples of **descriptive** writing? _____

5. Which are probably examples of **imaginative** writing? _____

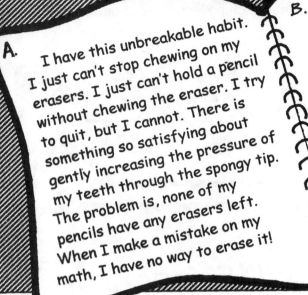

A.
I have this unbreakable habit.
I just can't stop chewing on my
erasers. I just can't hold a pencil
without chewing the eraser. I try
to quit, but I cannot. There is
something so satisfying about
gently increasing the pressure of
my teeth through the spongy tip.
The problem is, none of my
pencils have any erasers left.
When I make a mistake on my
math, I have no way to erase it!

B.
Eraser on my pencil top,
I chew on you and cannot stop.
How many times have you
been bit?
I try, but I just cannot quit.
As soon as one mistake's erased,
I hunger for your spongy taste.
My teeth dig in until they meet,
And soon you're lying at my feet.

6. Which piece of writing (above) is **prose**? Write the letter. _____

7. A form of writing that teaches a lesson or answers a question is a:

   a. legend   c. fable

   b. parody   d. proverb

8. A brief saying that states a general truth is a:

   a. myth   c. proverb

   b. ballad   d. fable

9. A form of writing that holds up human vices or follies to ridicule is a (an):

   a. satire   c. epic

   b. ode   d. parody

10. A form of writing that imitates the style of another work (usually for comic effect) is a (an):

    a. legend   c. editorial

    b. biography   d. parody

11. A preface or introduction to a literary work is a (an):

    a. epilogue   c. monologue

    b. prologue   d. dialogue

12. The continuation of a story begun in a previous work is a (an):

    a. prologue   c. sequel

    b. epitaph   d. spoof

13. Which piece of writing would probably NOT be descriptive?

    a. Yellow Pages ad

    b. weather report

    c. menu entry

    d. Wanted poster

    e. movie script

    f. movie review

Name _____

47

Writers use many different writing techniques and literary devices to make writing interesting.
Each of the sentences or phrases on the wall make use of different techniques.
Write the letter of each saying from the wall next to the matching technique or device listed below.

14. pun _____

15. simile_____

16. idiom_____

17. alliteration _____

18. personification _____

19. metaphor_____

20. hyperbole _____

21. onomatopoeia_____

Name _____

48

[1]The concert was sold out months ago. [2]Everybody in the city was wild about the hot new group, Rufus & the Razors. [3]We were so lucky to get tickets.

[4]The big night finally arrived. [5]And, oh what a disappointment! [6]This was not what we expected for the money we spent. [7]First of all, the seats were much farther from the stage than the brochure had promised. [8]Then the concert started two hours late. [9]This time was not added onto the end. [10]But the concert was so bad, who could have stood it any longer anyway? [11]The sound system screeched the whole time. [12]The group sang off tune. [13]Rufus was in a horrible mood. [14]He sang badly and, in between songs, he complained about the weather, the auditorium, and our city. [15]The group didn't even have time to sing their big hit song.

[16]What a letdown!

22. Circle statements that are true about this passage.
    a. The sentences vary in length.
    b. The sentences are all similar in length.
    c. The sentences are varied in structure.
    d. The sentences have similar structures.

23. Which sentences contain details that support the author's idea idea that the concert was disappointing?

    Write the numbers of the sentences: _____

24. What is the point of view of this selection?
    a. first person—narrator who is in the situation.
    b. second person—an outsider describing the situation.
    c. third person—an outsider describing what one character is thinking and experiencing.

25. This piece of writing is probably intended for:
    a. musicians
    b. teenagers
    c. guitar players
    d. music store owners

Name _____

Middle Grade Book of Language Tests

YELLOW

Yellow is BOLD.
Yellow never wants help,
But steps right out on its own,
Throwing bright light everywhere.
Yellow dashes through flower gardens,
Splashes on fried eggs,
Drips on traffic lights,
And wraps itself around bananas.
Yellow reaches out from the sun,
And never gives up.
Yellow is BOLD.

RED

Screeching sirens screaming,
Stoplights flashing,
Babies crying,
Spaghetti sauce bubbling.
Red stings your tongue with cinnamon,
And bites your nose with cold wind.
Red is angry tempers and words of fire
Like "loser!" "idiot!" or "liar!"
And red is embarrassment.

26. Which poem makes the most use of personification? _____

27. Write 5 verbs the writer uses to show the boldness of yellow.

_____

28. Write a line from that is effective in creating a visual image (from either poem).

_____

29. The RED poem appeals to _____ different senses. (Write a number.)

30. Circle the letters of the techniques used in the RED poem.
    a. rhyme
    b. repetition of lines
    c. satire
    d. personification
    e. appeal to sense of smell
    f. alliteration

31. The YELLOW poem appeals to _____ different senses. (Write a number.)

32. Circle the letters of the techniques used in the YELLOW poem.
    a. rhyme
    b. repetition of lines
    c. satire
    d. personification
    e. appeal to sense of smell
    f. alliteration

Name _____

WANTED: Responsible young rat is looking for house-sitting jobs. Available to take good care of your house and yard any evening or weekend. Experienced. References provided. Houses with good supply of cheese preferred. No homes with cats, please.

Contact Leroy at 663-0988 or email: leroyrat@rodent.com

CHEESE SOUFFLÉ

Start with 1 pound of good-quality cheddar cheese.
Shred the cheese finely. Set aside.
Whip 5 egg whites until stiff peaks form. Set aside.
Beat 5 egg yolks with ½ cup of milk.
Add ½ tsp of salt and ½ tsp of pepper.
Gently fold the beaten yolk mixture into the egg whites.
Gently fold in the shredded cheese.
Pour into a buttered 9 x 9 inch glass baking dish.
Bake for 35 minutes until puffy and golden.
Serve immediately.

MEETING NOTICE
The Lincoln School Board will hold its regular monthly meeting on Monday night at 7:00 p.m. in the district boardroom at 415 Grand Avenue. Agenda items include discussion of a school dress code, funding shortages, complaints about the transportation system, and the school lunch program. The public is welcome.

33. The writer probably wrote this ad to:

a. try to get some house-sitting jobs

b. meet some house-sitters

c. hire someone to take care of his house

d. make some new friends on the Internet

34. The purpose of this writing is to:

a. convince someone to make cheese soufflé

b. describe how cheese soufflé looks and tastes

c. instruct someone how to make cheese soufflé

d. show people that cheese soufflé has a lot of calories and fat

35. This meeting notice is intended for:

a. board members

b. the school superintendent

c. teachers

d. the general public

CONTENT & ORGANIZATION

Name _____   Possible Correct Answers: 50

Date _____   Your Correct Answers: _____

This test is made up of 10 writing tasks. You will be given a score of 1–5 points for each one, depending on how completely you follow the directions for the task.

Task # 1 WORD USE: Some words are missing from this description. Choose a fresh, interesting, and effective word or phrase to fill in each blank.

We were having a relaxing, _____ romp in the warm ocean waters. Not a care or a worry _____ any one of us. Suddenly, the peaceful scene was _____. A giant squid surfaced in our midst. With its _____eye and long, _____ tentacles, this strange creature _____ us. With _____ motions, we swam and raced for the beach, screaming all the way.

Task # 2 CLEAR SENTENCES: Write a sentence that accomplishes one of the goals below. Write the sentence in a way that expresses clearly what you mean to say.
- *Tell about an argument you lost.*
- *Reveal a wonderful secret.*
- *Describe a terribly silly event.*
- *Make a shocking announcement.*
- *Describe a dreadful feeling.*
- *Express a deep wish.*

Task # 3 INTERESTING SENTENCES: Choose a different topic from the Task # 2 box. Write one sentence that specifically has interesting sound, structure, and rhythm.

_____   _____

_____   _____

_____   _____

_____   _____

_____   _____

_____   _____

52

Task # 4 VARIED SENTENCES:
Write a paragraph that relates to this picture. Make sure that your sentences are varied in length and structure. Use at least 6 sentences.

Tell our readers what happened.

_____

_____

_____

_____

_____

_____

_____

_____

_____

Some curious fact-collectors have set out to find the extremes in weather on the earth. They have learned that the coldest inhabited place on earth is in northern Russia, while the hottest place is in the African country of Djibouti. An Arizona city registers the driest conditions of any inhabited place. The top sport for the wettest conditions in the inhabited world go to a city in Columbia, South America.

Task # 5 STRONG TITLES:
Write a good title or headline for each article or story. Make sure the headline (or title) is clearly a good label for the main idea of the piece.

A local farmer brought fame to the city of Brownsville this week. Elmer W. W. Growit's watermelon made a big impression at a nation-wide contest. The judging was held in Tuskegee, Alabama. Farmer Growit won the grand prize for the largest melon grown in the country. His watermelon weighed 165 pounds. When he returns to the county, he plans to invite 300 friends to help him eat the melon.

Name _____

TOPICS

- exploring King Tut's tomb
- a lost homework assignment
- a disturbing phone call
- writing a hit song
- an encounter with a scorpion
- a place to avoid
- a trip that didn't go well
- escape from a tidal wave
- a totally unexpected event
- a puzzling letter
- a cave adventure
- mystery in the city
- something worth forgetting
- a case of green earlobes

Task # 6 GREAT BEGINNINGS: Write a strong beginning for one of the topics. Make sure your beginning will grab the attention of the reader so he or she will want to read the whole piece of writing!

_____

_____

_____

Task # 7 STRONG ENDINGS: Write a strong ending for one of the topics. Make your ending effective, fresh, unusual, surprising, or shocking. It should be memorable—so that it will stay with the reader!

_____

_____

_____

Task # 8
CLEAR MAIN IDEA:

Write a letter expressing an opinion about one of these topics. Make sure that your letter contains a main point that you communicate clearly. When a reader finishes the letter, the main idea should be very clear.

- *something that should be changed*
- *something people should do every day*
- *something that really bothers you*
- *something you strongly support*
- *something that people should never do*
- *something that everybody needs*

Name

Task # 9 CLEAR ORGANIZATION:

Write a short description, tall tale, narrative story, imaginative story, argument, or speech to go along with this picture. Make sure your written work has:

- a strong beginning
- a clear and strong middle
- clear supporting details
- a clear sequence
- a memorable ending
- a good title

_____

_____

_____

_____

_____

_____

_____

_____

_____

_____

_____

_____

_____

_____

Name _____

Middle Grade Book of Language Tests

TASK # 10 GOOD DETAILS: Fill in the blank to finish the opening sentence of the essay. Then finish a good paragraph (or two) that contains at least five details or examples to support your first sentence. The details should make it clear to your reader why you would NOT want to visit this place. Give the essay a title.

_____

_____ *is a place I would rather not visit—not ever!*

_____

_____

_____

_____

_____

_____

_____

_____

_____

_____

_____

_____

_____

_____

_____

_____

I'm leaving!

EDITING

Name _____   Possible Correct Answers: 50

Date _____   Your Correct Answers: _____

This test is made up of 10 editing tasks. You will be given a score of 1–5 points for each one, depending on how completely you follow the directions for the task.

EDITING TASK # 1 IMPROVE WORD USE

1. **Replace each ordinary word in the passage with a more colorful or interesting word. Write the new word or phrase above each underlined word.**

> This is a tale of trouble—awful, **big**, trouble. It began when I **walked** into a **dark** corner behind the old garage. Right away, I knew I should have **gotten** out of there **quicker than a wink.**

2. **The sentences below do not have much action. Rewrite the sentences with active verbs.**

A. Is it true that you had fourteen tacos for breakfast?

_____

B. Last night's sunset seemed to be a brilliant one.

_____

C. The terrified hiker was able to get out of the path of Bigfoot.

_____

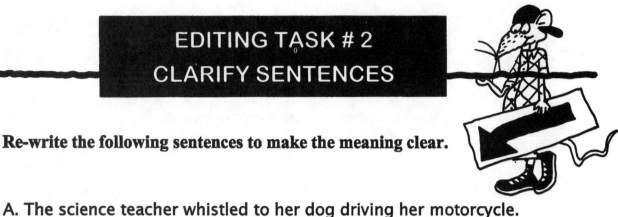

EDITING TASK # 2
CLARIFY SENTENCES

Re-write the following sentences to make the meaning clear.

A. The science teacher whistled to her dog driving her motorcycle.

_____

B. Riding my bike in the morning, the sun was getting hot.

_____

C. My sister told jokes while we were having the Johnson family for lunch.

_____

EDITING TASK # 3
IMPROVE SEQUENCE

These limericks do not make sense, because the ideas are not in a sensible sequence. Number the lines in each limerick so that the poem makes sense.

A.

____He felt really brave

____A spunky young fella named Pete

____Till he hit the first wave

____Decided to ski on his feet.

____Now he knows how to ski on his seat.

B.

____Yelled, "Hey, everyone, look at me!"

____Sky diver, Mickey McGee

____Now he's all tangled up in a tree.

____Not watching where he floated.

____He bragged and he gloated,

Name _____

Middle Grade Book of Language Tests

EDITING TASK # 4 ELIMINATE EXCESS WORDS

Cross out the words that are repetitive or not needed.

1. There were these three kids who came up with a plan to totally eat a whole cow.

2. Abby made a geometric design in math class that had three shapes: squares, three-sided triangles, and round circles.

3. In my opinion, I think that hang-gliding is not never a good idea.

EDITING TASK # 5 ELIMINATE EXCESS IDEAS

Read the passage. Cross out any sentences, phrases, or ideas that are not related to the topic.

Hello! Hello! Is this 9-1-1? I have an accident to report. I was driving west on Broadway in downtown when I witnessed a collision. I saw it all with my own eyes. A blue car and a red van were involved. There were two vehicles that hit each other. One car is on fire. I was on my way home from a movie. There were two people in the car. They got out. I think some people in the van are hurt. Both vehicles look very new. Please send an ambulance right away. The accident just happened. There might be someone injured. The accident is one block north of Jackson on Broadway. Just come to the intersection of Harvey and Broadway and it's right there. I have already eaten dinner. I can wait until the police arrive.

Revise each of these beginnings
to make them stronger
and more attention-getting for a reader.

EDITING
TASK # 6
STRENGTHEN
BEGINNINGS

1. It all began after we'd eaten ten pizzas.

_____

2. This is the story of an underwater adventure.

_____

3. Let me tell you why you shouldn't ride *The Cannonball Coaster.*

_____

EDITING
TASK # 7
STRENGTHEN
ENDINGS

Revise each of these endings
to make them more
effective and memorable.

1. And that is the end of the tale about the scorpion.

_____

2. It certainly was a mystery.

_____

3. So now you've heard my opinion about tattoos.

_____

Name _____

EDITING TASK # 8 STRENGTHEN TITLES

Replace the title with one that is more accurate and more interesting.

Accident in Sweetholm

An amusing event took place in the small town of Sweetholm this week. A disoriented driver intending to turn a corner mistakenly turned through the window of a bakery instead. Bakers and customers screamed as icing and doughnuts, pastries and whipped cream flew everywhere! Neighborhood children raced to the scene to gobble up the damaged goodies. The whole town came out to watch the excitement. Fortunately, no one was hurt in the accident.

EDITING TASK # 9 ADD DIALOGUE

Rewrite the passage so that it contains dialogue.

She ran to the police station and explained that the car had gone into the bakery through the window. She said that several people on the sidewalk screamed at the driver to stop, but it didn't help. She told the police that there were pastries and frosting everywhere. The police officer asked her name and address, and wrote down everything she said.

_____

_____

_____

_____

_____

_____

_____

_____

Name _____

EDITING TASK # 10
CORRECT ERRORS in CONVENTIONS

Fix the spelling, punctuation, capitalization, and grammar in this letter. Cross out the errors and write the corrections above each line.

January 15 2001

Dear editor

the situation with the parking, in the downtown area is abominable! Why don't the city councel do something about this? They are allowing more and more development. yet the parking is not growing to keep up with the trafic It is getting so that a person cannot stop to shop in the plaza area any longer. To make matters worse: the city they have just restricted 15 parking spaces in the busiest area. according to the sign these are now reserved for city vehicles City administrators, are you listening Your citazins are not happy about this.

sincerely,

Annoyed Andrew

WRITING PROCESS

Name _____

Possible Correct Answers: 30

Date _____

Your Correct Answers: _____

Your writing will be scored on these six traits.
You can receive 1 to 5 points on each trait.
A good piece of writing scores at least 3 points in each trait.

TRAITS

CONTENT:

The writing is clear and interesting and fun to read. The reader can easily understand the main point of the paper. You have used many details that grab the attention of the reader. You give information about your topic and clearly show what is happening.

WORD CHOICE:

The words are fresh and interesting. You have avoided overused, ordinary words. Your paper uses active verbs. You have used words and phrases that your reader will remember. The words strengthen your ideas and give them a good flavor.

VOICE:

The paper has your personal mark on it. It shows the feelings and personality of the writer. The reader can tell a human being wrote this paper. It talks directly to the reader and shows what you really think.

ORGANIZATION:

The paper starts with a catchy beginning. The writing builds to the important point, with plenty of connected details in a clear order. A reader will want to keep reading your paper. You avoid using a lot of unrelated ideas. Your paper has a good, memorable ending.

SENTENCES:

The sentences are clear and sound interesting. The sentences are different in length and structure. Your sentences do not all begin the same way. If you read your paper aloud, the sentences flow nicely together and sound smooth.

CONVENTIONS:

You have used punctuation and capitalization in the right places. Your spelling and grammar are correct. Each new idea is placed in a new paragraph.

DIRECTIONS

1) Choose ONE of the writing tasks below.
2) Use the space on page 3 to gather ideas about your topic.
3) Use page 3 to organize your ideas.
4) Use pages 4 and 5 to write a rough draft.
5) Use the *Editor's Guide* on page 6 to help you polish your writing.
6) Use pages 7 and 8 for your final draft.

STEP # 1: Choose One Writing Task

TASK # 1   Strange noises are heard in the sky over a neighborhood. Two friends go outside to investigate. **Make up a story** about what they found and about what happened to them. Include these words somewhere in the story:

"They could never have imagined what trouble would come from their curiosity."

TASK # 2   Think of a real or imaginary place. Convince your reader that it is a place they should **not** visit.

TASK # 3   **Describe** a character that you would like to meet. Explain what makes this character so interesting to you. The character may be real or imaginary.

TASK # 4   **Tell a true story** about an experience you hope **never** to have again.

TASK # 5   Think of something that you believe very strongly. **Explain** to a reader why you believe it, and why it is so important to you.

Name

65

Middle Grade Book of Language Tests

COLLECT IDEAS

Write down words, phrases, sentences, and ideas that you might want to include in your paper. Put down everything that comes to mind! You might not use it all, but keep brainstorming. Think of fresh and unusual ideas. Collect colorful words. Use another piece of paper if you need more space.

ORGANIZE IDEAS

Make an outline, web, or list to organize your ideas. Decide on a main idea for each paragraph. Pull together the ideas that support that idea.

Name

66

ROUGH DRAFT

_____

(Title)

_____

_____

_____

_____

_____

_____

_____

_____

_____

_____

_____

_____

_____

Name _____

ROUGH DRAFT, continued...

_____

_____

_____

_____

_____

_____

_____

_____

_____

_____

_____

_____

_____

_____

EDITOR'S GUIDE

CONTENT
___Does it make a clear main point that is easy to understand?
___Did I include examples or details that support the main point?
___Did I leave out details that don't relate to the main point?
___Does the paper show that I know something about the topic?
___Does it include fresh, interesting ideas?

ORGANIZATION
___Does it have a strong beginning that catches the reader's attention?
___Are the ideas written in an order that makes sense?
___Are the ideas that belong together grouped in the same paragraph?
___Will the reader want to keep on reading?
___Does the paper have a great, unusual ending?

WORD CHOICE
___Did I choose words that will capture the reader's imagination?
___Have I used some fresh, unusual, and colorful words or phrases?
___Have I used active verbs?
___Have I used words that make the meaning of the paper clear?

SENTENCES
___When I read the paper out loud, does it sound smooth?
___Are the sentences clear and interesting?
___Have I used different lengths of sentences?
___Have I used sentences that have different beginnings or structures?

VOICE
___Does my paper show personality?
___Does the writing show what I feel and think?
___Does the paper talk directly to the reader?

CONVENTIONS
___Have I used correct capitalization on sentences and names?
___Is my punctuation correct?
___Is my spelling correct?
___Have I used grammar correctly?
___Do all my paragraphs contain sentences on the same idea?
___Are all my paragraphs indented?

Name _____

FINAL DRAFT

_____

(Title)

_____

_____

_____

_____

_____

_____

_____

_____

_____

_____

_____

_____

_____

_____

_____

Name

Middle Grade Book of Language Tests

FINAL DRAFT, continued...

_____

_____

_____

_____

_____

_____

_____

_____

_____

_____

_____

_____

_____

_____

_____

_____

_____

STOP

Name _____

Grammar & Usage Skills Checklists

Grammar & Usage Test # 1:

PARTS OF SPEECH

Test Location: pages 75–81

Skill	Test Items
Recognize how a word is used in a sentence	1–17
Identify and distinguish between common and proper nouns	18, 19
Identify pronouns	20, 21
Identify and form singular and plural nouns	22–33
Identify and write plural possessive nouns correctly	34, 35, 37
Identify and write singular possessive nouns correctly	36, 38, 39, 40
Identify different kinds of pronouns (personal, possessive, indefinite, interrogative, and demonstrative)	41–45
Identify and distinguish between subject and object pronouns	46–49
Identify different verb tenses	50–55
Identify and use action and linking verbs	56–58, 63, 64
Distinguish between transitive and intransitive verbs	59–62
Identify regular and irregular verbs	65–67
Form verb tenses with regular and irregular verbs	68–75
Identify adjectives	76
Identify adverbs	77
Identify words modified by adjectives and adverbs	78, 79
Choose the correct form of a comparative or superlative adjective or adverb for a context	80–83
Identify and distinguish among gerunds, participles, and infinitives	84–90

Grammar & Usage Test # 2:

SENTENCES

Test Location: pages 82–85

Skill	*Test Items*
Identify and distinguish among complete sentences, sentence fragments, and run-on sentences	1–5
Identify and distinguish among declarative, imperative, exclamatory, and interrogative sentences	6–9
Identify and distinguish among simple, compound, and complex sentences	10–14
Identify the simple subject of a sentence	15–18
Identify the simple predicate of a sentence	19–22
identify the understood subject of a sentence	23, 24
Identify the complete subject of a sentence	25–28
Identify the complete predicate of a sentence	30–34
Identify sentences with compound subjects and predicates	29, 35
Identify predicate nouns and adjectives	36–39
Recognize the conjunction in a compound sentence	40–46
Create compound or complex sentences from simple sentences	47, 48
Rearrange words within a sentence for clear meaning	49, 50

Grammar & Usage Test # 3:

PHRASES & CLAUSES

Test Location: pages 86–89

Skill	*Test Items*
Recognize dangling and misplaced modifiers	1–8
Identify appositives	9–12
Recognize prepositional phrases	13
Recognize participial phrases	14
Recognize gerund phrases	15
Recognize infinitive phrases	16
Identify participles, prepositions, gerunds, and infinitives	17–20
Identify independent and subordinate clauses	21, 22
Identify essential and nonessential clauses	23, 24
Recognize and distinguish among noun clauses, adjective clauses, and adverb clauses	25–31
Recognize what a phrase modifies	32, 33
Recognize the correct use of who, whom, whoever, and whomever in phrases and clauses	34, 35

Middle Grade Book of Language Tests

Grammar & Usage Test # 4:

CAPITALIZATION & PUNCTUATION

Test Location: pages 90–93

Grammar & Usage Test # 5:

LANGUAGE USAGE

Test Location: pages 94–97

Middle Grade Book of Language Tests

PARTS OF SPEECH

Name _____

Possible Correct Answers: 90

Date _____

Your Correct Answers: _____

Identify the parts of speech in the sentence below by writing . . .

N for noun   **V** for verb   **AJ** for adjective   **AD** for adverb

> *Seventeen lighthouse keepers snored loudly every night.*

_____ 1. seventeen   _____ 3. keepers   _____ 5. loudly

_____ 2. lighthouse   _____ 4. snored   _____ 6. every   _____ 7. night

> *The yellow lights from the buoys flashed regularly throughout the night.*

_____ 8. yellow   _____ 9. lights   _____12. regularly

_____10. buoys   _____13. throughout

_____11. flashed   _____14. night

> *Never have I heard the moan of the foghorn as loud as it sounds tonight!*

15. Which words in the sentence above are used as nouns? _____

16. Which words are used as verbs? _____

17. Which words are used as adverbs? _____

18. Circle the **proper nouns** in this sentence (nouns that should be capitalized).

> The Grandville dive team left saturday for a summer-long trip to search for sunken treasure in the south atlantic ocean.

19. Circle the **common nouns** in this sentence.

> The captain should not let his ship, *The Lazy Skipper*, get caught near the dark waters of the Bermuda Triangle.

20. Circle the **pronouns** in this sentence.

> Her battered sailboat is old but it works better than yours.

21. Circle the **pronouns** in this sentence.

> She was chased by a shark, but they got there in time to rescue her from its jaws!

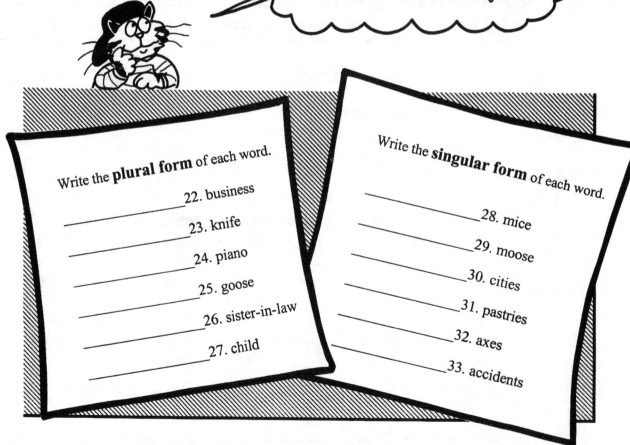

Write the **plural form** of each word.

_____ 22. business

_____ 23. knife

_____ 24. piano

_____ 25. goose

_____ 26. sister-in-law

_____ 27. child

Write the **singular form** of each word.

_____ 28. mice

_____ 29. moose

_____ 30. cities

_____ 31. pastries

_____ 32. axes

_____ 33. accidents

34. the surfboards belonging to two monkeys

35. the swimsuits belonging to five girls

36. goggles belonging to the swimmer

37. the appetites of the lifeguards

38. the tentacles of the octopus

39. the pet jellyfish of Mr. Zax

40. raft belonging to Spike

Write a **possessive noun phrase**
(2 words) to fit each description.

34. _____

35. _____

36. _____

37. _____

38. _____

39. _____

40. _____

Identify the different kinds of pronouns.

41. Circle the **personal pronoun**: We will enjoy eating their picnic food.

42. Circle the **possessive pronoun**: Which shark's tooth is mine?

43. Circle the **indefinite pronoun**: Others will want to rent skis today because it is sunny.

44. Circle the **interrogative pronoun**: Which jet ski do you want: this one or that one?

45. Circle the **demonstrative pronoun**: I don't want to buy those, but someone else might.

46. **Did the giant squid chase you or her?**

    You and her are: a. subject pronouns   b. object pronouns

47. **Those are not sea anemones; these are!**

    Those and these are: a. subject pronouns   b. object pronouns

48. **Yesterday, they swam out to the buoy and back ten times.**

    They is: a. subject pronoun   b. object pronoun

49. **When the boat quit working, Leroy left it and swam for shore.**

    It is: a. subject pronoun   b. object pronoun

Choose the form of the verb *pinch* that is described.

50. **paste tense:**
   a. pinches
   b. will pinch
   c. pinched

51. **present tense:**
   a. pinched
   b. will pinch
   c. pinch

52. **future tense:**
   a. is pinching
   b. will pinch
   c. pinched

53. **past perfect tense:**
   a. has pinched
   b. had pinched
   c. will have pinched

54. **present perfect tense:**
   a. has pinched
   b. had pinched
   c. will have pinched

55. **future perfect tense**
   a. has pinched
   b. had pinched
   c. will have pinched

In the next 3 sentences, tell whether the verb is an **action verb** or a **linking verb**. Write A or L.

_____56. Spike has a mouth full of salt water.

_____57. Spike swallowed a mouth full of seaweed.

_____58. Spike is becoming weary of drinking seawater.

In the next 4 sentences, tell whether the verb is **transitive** or **intransitive**. Write T or I.

_____59. Which divers explored the sunken submarine?

_____60. Did the sunken treasure look valuable?

_____61. Watch out for sharks!

_____62. Lifeguards posted signs along the beach.

63. Circle an **action verb**: He thought the shark was menacing.

64. Circle a **linking verb**: Leroy said to his friend, "Your fish sandwich seems tasty."

Name _____

Middle Grade Book of Language Tests

65. Circle the **regular verbs** on the note.

I am lost at sea. I left on June, 14, 1998. I began my trip
in Miami and sailed toward Bimini. My ship was dashed
on the rocks near an uncharted island.
I have escaped from sharks and pirates. Please help!
Signed, Sandy Sandlogged

66. Circle the **irregular verbs** on the note.

Help me, please! I was lucky enough
to write this note and send it floating off just
as a whale swallowed me. He ate me right up while
I was floating on my raft. If you find a large white
whale, please look inside for poor me.
Hurry, Andy Credible

67. Circle the **irregular verbs** on the note.

If you find this note, please come and look for me.
I built a raft and rode it across the bay
until I fell off. Huge seagulls plucked me
from the water and flew me to this unknown island.
I wrote this note on a seagull's wing. Help!
Lonely me, Harry Floatman

Name

79

Write each of these verbs in its **past tense**.

_____ 68. swim

_____ 69. dive

_____ 70. take

_____ 71. bring

Write each of these verbs in its **present tense**.

_____ 72. worried

_____ 73. went

_____ 74. broke

_____ 75. wrote

76. Circle the words that are used as **adjectives**.

> Six mischievous kids boiled up Mrs. O'Grady's pet lobster and ate him for lunch.

77. Circle the words that are used as **adverbs**.

> Totally outraged by this, Mrs. O'Grady promptly dumped their snorkel gear off the pier.

78. In the sentences above, which word is modified by **six**?_____

79. In the sentences above, which word is modified by **promptly**?_____

Choose the correct form of the **adjective** or **adverb** to fit in the blank.

80. Leroy thinks the octopus is the _____ of all the sea creatures.

    a. scarier   b. scariest   c. more scary   d. scary

81. Spike is a bad diver, but his brother is even _____.

    a. worst   b. more worse   c. worse   d. more worst

82. That is the _____ surf on the whole coast.

    a. most dangerous   b. more dangerous   c dangerouser

83. Chichi thinks she can catch that big wave _____than the other surfers.

    a. easier   b. more easy   c. more easily   d. most easily

Name _____

80

84. In which sentence is *surfing* used as a **gerund**?

   a. Leroy's surfing friends dragged themselves out of the icy water.

   b. Is surfing Leroy's favorite way to avoid homework?

   c. Leroy and his friends go surfing several times a week.

Read the signs.

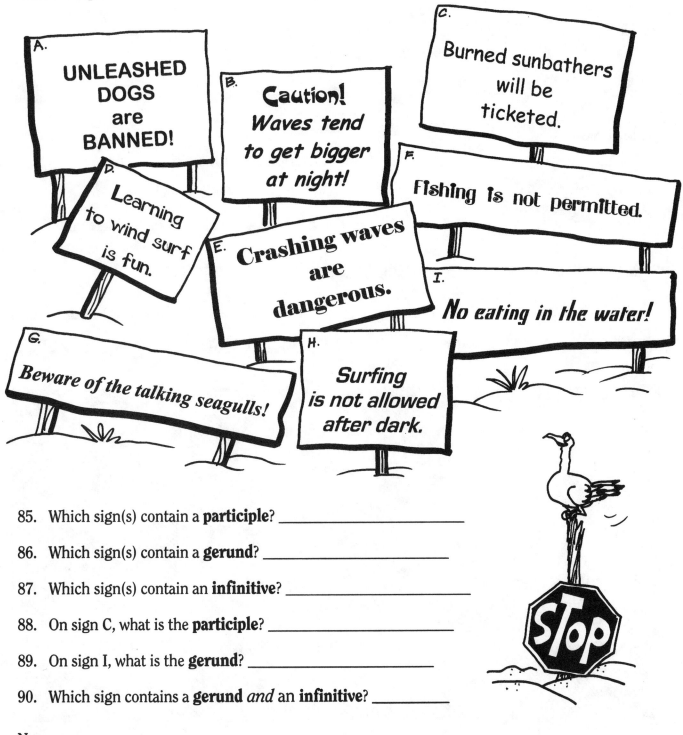

A. UNLEASHED DOGS are BANNED!

B. Caution! Waves tend to get bigger at night!

C. Burned sunbathers will be ticketed.

D. Learning to wind surf is fun.

E. Crashing waves are dangerous.

F. Fishing is not permitted.

G. Beware of the talking seagulls!

H. Surfing is not allowed after dark.

I. No eating in the water!

85. Which sign(s) contain a **participle**? _____

86. Which sign(s) contain a **gerund**? _____

87. Which sign(s) contain an **infinitive**? _____

88. On sign C, what is the **participle**? _____

89. On sign I, what is the **gerund**? _____

90. Which sign contains a **gerund** *and* an **infinitive**? _____

Name _____

SENTENCES

Name _____

Possible Correct Answers: 50

Date _____

Your Correct Answers: _____

Decide if each group of words is a complete sentence, a sentence fragment, or a run-on sentence. Write **C** (*for complete*), **F** (*for fragment*), or **R** (*for run-on*).

_____ 1. Chichi stayed inside all day she had a terrible sunburn.

_____ 2. Because of her severe sunburn.

_____ 3. Feeling miserable, Chichi stayed inside.

_____ 4. Never having been burned so badly before.

_____ 5. Wouldn't it be a good idea to use sunscreen?

Examine each quote below. Decide what kind of sentence it is.

6. Which sentences are declarative? _____

7. Which sentences are exclamatory? _____

8. Which ones are imperative? _____

9. Which ones are interrogative? _____

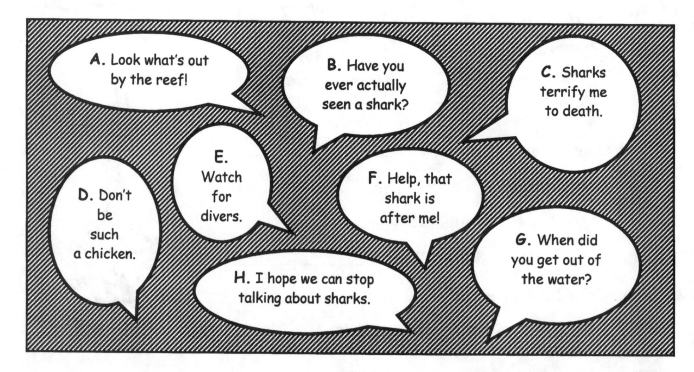

Write **S**   for simple sentence,
    C   for compound sentence,
    CX   for complex sentence.

_____10. We took our chances.

_____11. We took a chance, and, oh, were we sorry!

_____12. Knowing it might be dangerous, we took a chance and swam to the pier.

_____13. Mermaids might appear during the day and sea monsters might appear at night.

_____14. Before you look for a mermaid, read this story.

Write the **simple subject** for each sentence

_____15. The blue-ringed octopus is a deadly creature.

_____16. Can those submarines really get to the bottom?

_____17. Underwater volcanoes erupt all the time.

_____18. Who is searching for the lost city of Atlantis?

Write the **simple predicate** for each sentence.

_____19. Look for the whip-like tail on the stingrays.

_____20. It all happened just before the big storm.

_____21. Signs reminded us not to touch the coral reef.

_____22. Try to float with your knees up.

Write the **understood subject** for each sentence.

_____23. Watch out for the undertow!

_____24. Stay away from the Bermuda Triangle.

Name _____

Middle Grade Book of Language Tests

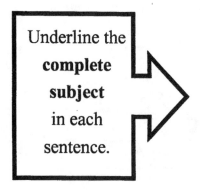

Underline the **complete subject** in each sentence.

25. Seven fierce pirates floated on their backs in the calm water.

26. My new underwater camera and flippers were a waste of money.

27. The long blue whale, which eats millions of shrimp, just swam by.

28. A prickly sea urchin is not a good thing to pick up.

29. Which sentence above has a **compound subject**?_____

30. Cold, tired, and cranky from a hard day at sea, Mr. Grumbly slept.

31. Sailors on a dozen boats are eating fresh fish tonight.

32. Would you go sailing during a hurricane?

33. You should never put a sea cucumber in a salad.

34. The clever puffer fish inflates itself and makes itself look scary.

35. Which sentence above has a **compound predicate**?_____

Underline the **complete predicate** in each sentence.

36. Which word in the sentence is a **predicate noun**?_____

Shrimp and small fish are food for whales.

37. Which word in the sentence is a **predicate noun**?_____

The storm eventually became a monster.

38. Which word in the sentence is a **predicate adjective**?_____

Seaweed feels slimy against my skin.

39. Which word in the sentence is a **predicate adjective**?_____

To most of the hungry guests, the chowder tasted delicious.

Name _____

Middle Grade Book of Language Tests

40. Butch couldn't be a lifeguard because he's afraid of water.

41. The swimmers get nervous whenever they hear reports of sharks.

42. We ended up on a desert island after our ship sank.

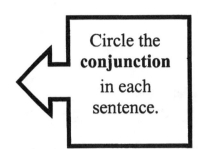

Circle the
conjunction
in each
sentence.

43. Chichi has been very sick since she ate all that sand.

44. Of course I could swim 20 miles, but I don't want to.

45. The picnic was fun, although it started late.

46. Did you see any pirates or find any buried treasure?

47. Write one **clear compound** or **complex sentence** by joining the two simple sentences.

Fred and Ned are brothers. Fred and Ned are terrified of crabs.

_____

48. Write one **clear compound** or **complex sentence** by joining the two simple sentences.

The sand was so hot.   It burned my feet badly.

_____

Re-write each sentence so that the **meaning is clear**.

49. While sailing my boat, a fish jumped up and bit me.

_____

_____

50. I heard about a diver who got cornered by a shark on the radio.

_____

_____

Name _____

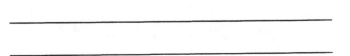

85

PHRASES & CLAUSES

Name _____　　　Possible Correct Answers: 35

Date _____　　　Your Correct Answers: _____

Which sentences below have
a **dangling or misplaced modifier**?
Write **X** next to each one that does.

_____1. After sailing all day, a lunch was served.

_____2. While floating on my raft, a jellyfish stung me.

_____3. Spike filmed fish holding his underwater camera.

_____4. Leroy read a book suntanning on his beach chair.

_____5. Spike answered his cell phone climbing on board his sailboat.

_____6. Chicken was served to the surfers covered with barbecue sauce.

_____7. We all wrote stories about surfing for an assignment at school.

_____8. While she waited for the next wave, Chichi rested on her surfboard.

Circle the
appositive in
each sentence.

9. Spike's dad, a lifeguard, swims ten miles a day in the ocean.

10. They went diving near the Great Barrier Reef, the world's largest reef.

11. Where can they see an African giant snail, the largest snail in the world?

12. The Portuguese Man-O-War, a floating colony of jellyfish, has about 500,000 stingers.

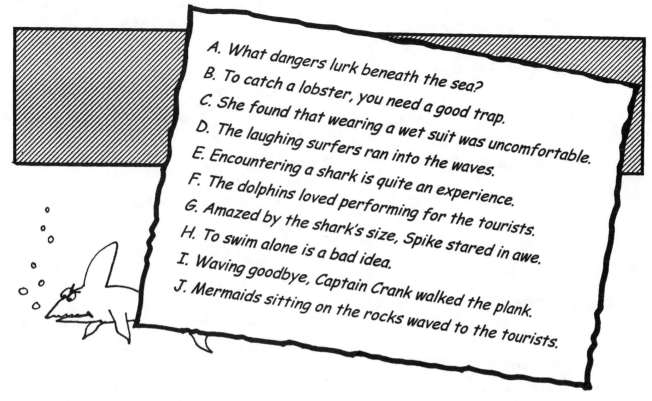

A. What dangers lurk beneath the sea?
B. To catch a lobster, you need a good trap.
C. She found that wearing a wet suit was uncomfortable.
D. The laughing surfers ran into the waves.
E. Encountering a shark is quite an experience.
F. The dolphins loved performing for the tourists.
G. Amazed by the shark's size, Spike stared in awe.
H. To swim alone is a bad idea.
I. Waving goodbye, Captain Crank walked the plank.
J. Mermaids sitting on the rocks waved to the tourists.

13. Which of these sentences have **prepositional phrases**? (one or more.)_____

14. Which of these sentences have **participial phrases**? (one or more.)_____

15. Which of these sentences have **gerund phrases**? (one or more.)_____

16. Which of these sentences have **infinitive phrases**? (one or more.)_____

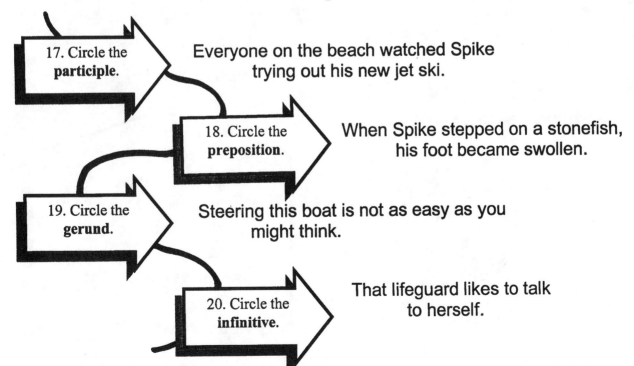

17. Circle the **participle**.

Everyone on the beach watched Spike
trying out his new jet ski.

18. Circle the **preposition**.

When Spike stepped on a stonefish,
his foot became swollen.

19. Circle the **gerund**.

Steering this boat is not as easy as you
might think.

20. Circle the **infinitive**.

That lifeguard likes to talk
to herself.

They stayed behind the reef until the barracuda passed.

21. What is the **independent clause**?

A. behind the reef
B. They stayed behind the reef
C. until the barracuda passed
D. the barracuda passed

We're asking you to get the hot dogs because we're lazy and tired.

22. What is the **subordinate clause**?

A. get the hot dogs
B. We're asking you
C. lazy and tired
D. because we're lazy and tired

The great white shark, the largest of all sharks, has four rows of teeth.

23. What is the **nonessential clause**?

A. The great white shark
B. the largest of all sharks
C. of all sharks
D. has four rows of teeth

Though they seemed brave, the divers panicked at the sight of the eel.

24. What is the **essential clause**?

A. Though they seemed brave
B. the divers panicked
C. at the sight of the eel
D. the divers panicked at the sight of the eel

Name _____

Middle Grade Book of Language Tests

Circle a clause in each sentence. Write the letters to show what kind of clause it is.
Write N for noun clause, ADJ for adjective clause, and ADV for adverb clause.

_____25. Those who are diving today get a free lunch.

_____26. Whoever comes along on the dive will have fun.

_____27. She screamed as if a whale was swallowing her.

_____28. Lolly is the diver who is the owner of the red mask.

_____29. Before I dive, I want to make sure there are no sharks.

_____30. When I dive near a sunken ship, I feel a sense of mystery.

_____31. Anyone could join the scuba class, which began last week.

32. In sentence 28 (above), what word is modified by

the phrase, *who is the owner of the red mask*?_____

33. In sentence 31 (above), what word is modified by

the phrase, *which began last week*?_____

34. Circle the letter if the sentence uses *who* or *whom* correctly.

A. Remind me whom I scheduled to lifeguard today.

B. She is the lifeguard who saved that cute little rat yesterday.

C. Spike, who rescued three dogs today, has excellent life guarding skills.

D. He is a lifeguard to whom I complained yesterday.

E. Buster is a lifeguard whom never leaves his chair.

35. Circle the letter if the sentence uses *whoever* or *whomever* correctly.

A. Whoever hired Sparky to be a lifeguard?

B. Whomever Spike rescued called him a hero.

C. Give the Lifeguard-of-the-Year Award to whomever deserves it.

D. Buy some ice cream for whoever wants it!

Name _____ **89** _____

CAPITALIZATION & PUNCTUATION

Name _____

Date _____

Possible Correct Answers: 40

Your Correct Answers: _____

Correct the **capitalization and punctuation** on this letter and envelope.
Write capital letters over incorrect letters. Add punctuation marks where they are needed.
Write correct punctuation marks over incorrect ones. *There are 18 errors.*

june 16 2001

dear rita

You should see me water-ski! I am awesome
at dozens of tricks. Really, I am! Last week,
I was in my first ski-jump contest. I gave the
spectators a great thrill. I'm sure they'll
remember my performance for a long time.

Although I promised to visit you next week,
I will be staying home for a while. This sport
of mine takes a lot of time. Maybe I'll be able
to see you in a few months.

sincerely

Leroy

leroy leroux
1414 west end ave.
cheesetown OR 95555

Cousin Rita R. Rat
6000 vermin boulevard
rodentville MA 00312

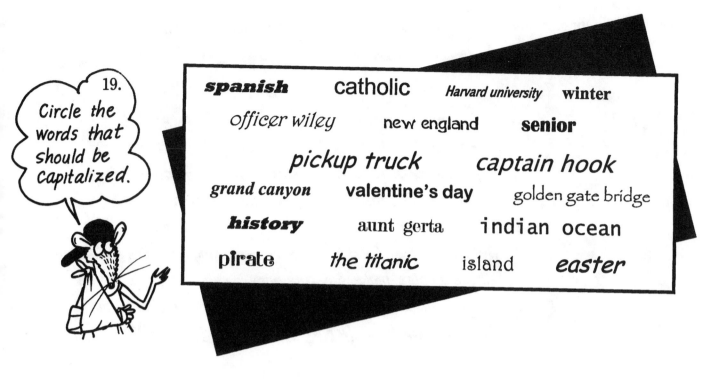

19. Circle the words that should be capitalized.

spanish   catholic   *Harvard university*   winter

officer wiley   new england   **senior**

pickup truck   captain hook

grand canyon   **valentine's day**   golden gate bridge

history   aunt gerta   indian ocean

pirate   *the titanic*   island   *easter*

20. Circle the words in this sentence that should have **capital letters**.
We could see Jupiter and the big dipper from zuma beach last summer.

21. Which sentences have correct **capitalization**? Circle the letters.
   a. Don't you prefer sailing the Caribbean sea to driving the Pennsylvania turnpike?
   b. Spike and Chichi could see Catalina Island from their boat, *The Happy Skipper*.
   c. Is Crater Lake the deepest body of water in the United States?
   d. Other than the shipwreck last Sunday, how was your Cruise of the Greek Islands?

22. Which sentences show correct **use of commas**? Circle the letters.
   a. I'm sure however that the tide won't be high until midnight.
   b. Hey, have you spotted any sharks today, Spike?
   c. Startled by a barracuda, Leroy swam back to shore in record time.
   d. Spike does not eat clams nor does he eat crab.

23. Which sentences show correct **use of commas**? Circle the letters.
   a. Blackbeard, the fierce pirate, left some treasure in this area.
   b. On Thursday August 15, 2000, we visited Sea World with 120000 others.
   c. An ornery hungry whale kept hanging around our boat.
   d. A good seafood stew must contain lobster, scallops, shrimp, clams, and fresh fish.

Name

91

24. Which sentences in Spike's list have **correct punctuation**? Circle the letters.

THINGS TO DO BEFORE THE TRIP

A. Make appointment with foot doctor Dr. J. D. Arch M. D.

B. Make a call to all the sailors who are (going on the trip.)

C. Buy these boat supplies; bandages, water, paint, and food.

D. Clean the life preservers; they need a good scrubbing.

E. Find Gigi's wet suit. (She claims an octopus ate it.)

F. Get some great food for the trip—hot dogs, ice cream, and pizza.

G. Above all else, make sure the boat is ready to sail at 6:30.

H. Lester—an excellent sailor—should come along; call him.

I. Take that new book, <u>Danger on the High Seas</u> (1999).

25. Circle the contractions that have **correct punctuation**.

won't	aren't	I'm
youv'e	you're	is'nt
they'll		was'nt
	shouldv'e	don't
can't	wer'e	they're

A. the lifeguard's suntan

B. the childrens's blanket

C. two swimmer's goggles

D. ten lobsters' claws

E. a seagull's footprints

F. the ship's deck

G. nine sailors' stomachaches

26. Circle the titles that have **correct capitalization**.

A. The Old man and the Sea

B. Once Upon An Innertube

C. Learn Lifeguarding Skills

D. Much Ado About Waves

E. Underwater Monsters and Mysteries

F. Learn to Surf in a Backyard Pool

G. The Secret Art of sand sculptures

thirty-two	mother-in-law
ice-cream	well-known
one-half	French-fries
stomach-ache	sea-shell
up-to-the-minute report	

27. Circle the possessive phrases that have **correct punctuation**.

28. Circle the words that show **correct use of hyphens**.

Name _____

Circle the letter of the sentence that shows correct **capitalization and punctuation**.

29.

a. "I really did see a mermaid, Spike tried to convince his friends."

b. " I really did see a mermaid," Spike tried to convince his friends.

c. " I really did see a mermaid," Spike, "tried to convince his friends."

30.

30. a. "No way!" laughed Buster. "There is no such thing as a mermaid!"

b. "No way, laughed Buster, "there is no such thing as a mermaid!"

c. "No way, laughed Buster, there is no such thing as a mermaid!"

31.

a. "Rufus asked," did she have a long, scaly green tail?

b. Rufus asked, "did she have a long, scaly green tail?"

c. Rufus asked, "Did she have a long, scaly green tail?"

32.

a. "You guys are making fun of me." complained Spike.

b. "You guys are making fun of me" complained Spike.

c. "You guys are making fun of me," complained Spike.

33.

a. "Well, you might be interested to know," interrupted Gigi, "that I am a mermaid."

b. "Well, you might be interested to know interrupted Gigi," that I am a mermaid.

c. "Well, you might be interested to know," interrupted Gigi, "That I am a mermaid."

Correct the **capitalization and punctuation errors** in the sentences below. Add punctuation where it is needed. Cross out and replace incorrect letters or punctuation marks.

34. Heres what I heard from an old Sea captain: reef sharks are more friendly than barracudas.

35. Last summer we sailed past the Statue of liberty in new york: it was exciting!

36. nine sting rays surrounded my Sister as she swam in the Atlantic ocean

37. do Lobsters live in the Mississippi River or in the San Francisco bay.

38. The storm—it lasted four hours: left dozens of uprooted trees.

39. The largest Island, in the world, is Australia.

40. Spikes nose was sunburned by 315 in the Afternoon.

Name _____

Middle Grade Book of Language Tests

LANGUAGE USAGE

Name _____

Date _____

Possible Correct Answers: 50

Your Correct Answers: _____

Circle the **correct form of the verb** to agree with the subject of the sentence.

1. Fish and small children (eat, eats) worms.

2. Hurricanes regularly (hit, hits) this part of the coast.

3. News of Spike's surfing accident (spread, spreads) quickly.

4. Neither Spike nor Leroy (surf, surfs) in waves this dangerous.

5. Several coconuts (fall, falls) from these palm trees every day.

6. Is it true that giant spider crabs (have, has) a 12-foot claw span?

7. The claws of lobsters and crabs (give, gives) them a bad reputation.

8. Every team in the beach volleyball competition (think, thinks) they will win.

Choose the **correct pronoun** to agree with the noun.

9. Those pesky sharks keep showing (their, its) fins.

10. Did Spike or Leroy lose (his, their) swimsuit in that big wave?

11. Gigi's sunscreen is old, so (it, she) probably won't work very well.

12. The dolphins and the whales put on a good show for (its, their) audience.

Choose the **correct pronoun** for each blank. Circle the pronoun.

13. _____ was the surprise guest at the beach party? (Who, Whom)

14. I think I know _____ planned this wild party. (who, whom)

15. _____ comes will have a grand time! (Whoever, whomever)

16. To _____ did you send invitations, anyway? (who, whom)

17. I sent them to _____ was on the list you gave me. (whoever, whomever)

18. Which is correct?

a. Could you borrow a raft from he and she?

b. Could you borrow a raft from him and her?

c. Could you borrow a raft from he and her?

d. Could you borrow a raft from him and she?

19. Which is correct?

a. Me and him already have a raft.

b. Him and I already have a raft.

c. I and he already have a raft.

d. He and I already have a raft

Circle the correct pronoun or pair of pronouns for each sentence.

20. The stingrays are staying away from (we, us,) girls.

21. Yesterday, (we, us) kids swam with some dolphins.

22. Spike and Buster can ski better than (they, them).

23. Cici stayed on the beach; we like exploring the sandbar better than (she, her).

24. (Her, She) and Mimi have never found sand dollars with us.

25. Please ask (her and them, she and they) not to eat our candy while we're swimming.

26. Don't you want to have a dolphin ride with (him and I, him and me, he and I)?

27. Circle the letters of the sentences that use negatives incorrectly.

A. Scarcely nobody swims here.

B. No camping is ever allowed on the beach.

C. We don't allow no fishing neither.

D. You won't find any riptides in this area.

E. Buried treasure hasn't ever been found here.

F. There aren't hardly any starfish on this beach.

G. You shouldn't take no shells off this beach.

H. Don't feed anything to the seagulls.

I. Don't never have a beach picnic without marshmallows.

Name _____

Every sentence has an error in language usage.
Find the error, cross it out, and fix the sentence so the **usage is correct**.

28. Did you rise the flag before the sun came up?

29. Not everyone can surf as good as Spike!

30. You would of screamed, too, if you had been that close to a killer whale.

31. Seven sick sailors laid moaning on the deck.

32. What caused Cici to raise up from her beach towel?

33. Don't sit your swim mask down on the sand.

34. Isn't it well that the sharks are not biting today?

35. Isn't it lucky that Leroy he got away from the shark?

36. Let's set on our chairs and get a tan.

37. I can learn you how to water-ski in one lesson!

38. Let's leave everyone sleep on the sand.

39. Can I please borrow your snorkel?

40. How long have you laid in this hot sun?

41. You did good to survive that dive!

42. Did you lie these sandals on my towel?

Middle Grade Book of Language Tests

43. Leroy has written some sentences about the day at the beach.
Check his usage of these words: *bad* and *badly*, *beside* and *besides*, *farther* and *further*, *real* and *really*, *between* and *among*, *sure* and *surely*. and *quick* and *quickly*.

Circle the letters of the sentences that show correct usage.

A. Look out for that eel swimming besides you!

B. Is anyone else frightened as bad as I am?

C. It's no wonder my stomach is feeling rather bad right now.

D. Which is farther away, the whale or the shark?

E. A swimmer is caught among the whale and the shark.

F. Somebody besides Cici needs to rescue that poor swimmer.

G. We saw the lifeguard raise up quickly out of her chair.

H. A lifeguard will sure get to the swimmer on time.

I. Look at how badly Leroy is sunburned today!

J. His friend, Butch, has a really bad sunburn, too.

K. Did you get much further in your book about jellyfish?

Circle the object in each sentence. Is it used as a direct object or indirect object?
Write D for direct and I for indirect.

_____44. The lifeguard signaled Spike a warning.

_____45. Today, a shark ate someone's snorkel.

_____46. Yesterday, a barracuda chased the diver.

_____47. Who sent my boyfriend a letter in a bottle?

_____48. Cici handed her friend, Mimi, a hermit crab.

_____49. Did Spike eat all the clam chowder?

_____50. Which pirate showed you the buried treasure?

Name _____

Middle Grade Book of Language Tests

Vocabulary & Word Skills Checklists

Vocabulary & Word Skills Test # 1:
WORD PARTS

Test Location: pages 100–103

Skill	Test Items
Recognize the meanings of common prefixes	1–12
Use knowledge of prefixes to determine word meaning	13–28
Recognize the meanings of common suffixes	29–38
Use suffixes to determine word meaning	39–52
Identify the meanings of common roots	53–68
Use knowledge of prefixes, suffixes, and roots to write words that match a meaning	69–71
Use knowledge of prefixes and suffixes to determine word meaning	72–76
Identify compound words	77–80

Vocabulary & Word Skills Test # 2:
VOCABULARY WORD MEANINGS

Test Location: pages 104–109

Skill	Test Items
Show understanding of word meaning by answering questions about word use	1–25
Use context clues to determine a word's meaning	26–30
Distinguish between the denotation and connotation of a word	31–33
Identify a word from its denotation and connotation	34–35
Choose a word of the correct connotation for a context	36–37
Recognize synonyms	38–42
Recognize antonyms	43–47
Identify words with similar meanings	48–51
Choose the correct word for a particular context	52–56
Recognize the multiple meanings of a word	57–60

Vocabulary & Word Skills Test # 3:

CONFUSING WORDS

Test Location: pages 110–113

Copyright ©2001 by Incentive Publications, Inc., Nashville, TN.

Middle Grade Book of Language Tests

WORD PARTS

Name _____   Possible Correct Answers: 80

Date _____   Your Correct Answers: _____

---

transmit	**supersonic**
malpractice	**reorganize**
hemisphere	**antidote**
subnormal	**exit**
universe	**maximum**
improper	**prepare**

Write the word from the sign that has a **prefix** meaning . . .

1. large or most _____

2. across _____

3. against _____

4. not _____

5. wrong _____

6. one _____

7. below _____

8. again _____

9. above or beyond _____

10. before _____

11. out _____

12. half _____

Add a **prefix** to form a word that fits the meaning.

13. _____ legible   (*not readable*)

14. _____ stress   (*against stress*)

15. _____ angle   (*having 4 angles*)

16. _____ pel   (*throw out*)

17. _____ mobile   (*move by itself*)

18. _____ represent   (*represent wrongly*)

19. _____ meter   (*1000 meters*)

20. _____ trust   (*not trust*)

21. _____ operate   (*operate together*)

22. _____ gon   (*7-sided figure*)

23. _____ active   (*extra active*)

24. _____ sensitive   (*not sensitive*)

25. _____ cultural   (*across cultures*)

26. _____ moral   (*without morals*)

27. _____ date   (*put a later date*)

28. _____ circle   (*half a circle*)

100

Write the word from the sign that has a **suffix** meaning . . . .

29. one who _____

30. without _____

31. full of _____

32. belonging to _____

33. able to be _____

34. made of _____

35. towards _____

36. the condition of _____

37. resembling_____

38. to make _____

backwards
dangerous
magnify
foolish
terrorist
clarity
Canadian
hopeless
edible
wooden

Add a **suffix** to form a word that fits the meaning.

39. (*like a sphere*)   spher_____

40. (*full of wind*)   wind _____

41. (*without spots*)   spot _____

42. (*toward the sea*)   sea _____

43. (*one who acts*)   act _____

44. (*made of silk*)   silk _____

45. (*resembling a child*)   child _____

46. (*small pigs*)   pig_____

47. (*to make weak*)   weak _____

48. (*one who begs*)   beg_____

49. (*like a fool*)   fool _____

50. (*to make fertile*)   fertil_____

51. (*full of slander*)   slander_____

52. (*one who presides*)   presid_____

This way to the Amusement Park

Middle Grade Book of Language Tests

synonym

gravity   laboratory

suspend   journal   dormitory

dynamite   astronomy   torture   altitude

tactile   chronological   projectile

translucent   auditorium

applaud

Find a word on the sign whose **root** matches each of these meanings. Write the word.

53. high _____

54. throw _____

55. sound _____

56. touch _____

57. heavy _____

58. praise _____

59. light _____

60. work _____

61. hang _____

62. time _____

63. day _____

64. twist _____

65. power _____

66. same _____

67. star _____

68. sleep _____

Write a word to match each meaning.
Use your knowledge of prefixes, suffixes, and roots.

69. study of the earth _____

70. not able to be bent _____

71. one who governs _____

Name _____

Circle the answers.

72. Which word means *beyond natural*?

internatural

supernatural

subnatural

hyponatural

73. Which word means *to climb up*?

descend

ascend

nonsense

decency

74. Which word means *the act of electing*?

election

elector

electable

electric

75. Which word means *in a tender manner*?

tenderness

tenderize

intention

tenderly

76. Which word means *one who causes terror*?

terrible

terrify

terrorist

terrorism

Which words in each group are NOT **compound words**? Cross them out.

77.
whiplash
stomachache
outrage
subtract
perilous
octopus
oceanography

78.
superjet
boycott
sunlight
hurricane
subconscious
friendly
baseball

79.
headache
outdoors
seasick
sailor
transatlantic
forecast
megaphone

80.
sunburn
backyard
afternoon
sunset
hyperactive
nonsense
quicksand

Name _____

VOCABULARY WORD MEANINGS

Name _____

Possible Correct Answers: 60

Date _____

Your Correct Answers: _____

Circle the most reasonable answer (**yes** or **no**).

1. Could a ride on a roller coaster produce **nausea**?　　**yes**　**no**

2. Could you be attacked by a **gargoyle**?　　**yes**　**no**

3. Should you destroy a **hallowed** object?　　**yes**　**no**

4. Is a **boycott** similar to an apricot?　　**yes**　**no**

5. Could you feed a melon to a **felon**?　　**yes**　**no**

6. Could you **ingest** a cream puff?　　**yes**　**no**

7. Would an **annuity** probably be tasty?　　**yes**　**no**

8. Could you style your hair with a **catacomb**?　　**yes**　**no**

9. Would you keep a **gazette** in the refrigerator?　　**yes**　**no**

10. Could a **tycoon** get caught in a **typhoon**?　　**yes**　**no**

11. Could a **biped** ride a bicycle?　　**yes**　**no**

12. If you had a terrible headache, would you want to be around a **garrulous** person?　　**yes**　**no**

Circle the most reasonable answer.

13. What would you do with
    an **heirloom**?
    bake it
    treasure it
    water it
    dance to it

14. What would you do with
    an **incisor**?
    put it in the bank
    sing to it
    brush it
    swat it

15. What would you do with
    a **soufflé**?
    send it to school
    draw with it
    hire it
    eat it

16. What would you do with
    a **ragamuffin**?
    feed it
    put it in a jewelry box
    paint it
    eat it

17. What would you do with
    a **garnish**?
    go swimming with it
    put it on a salad
    take it to the library
    put it in your ears

18. Where would you find
    a **villain**?
    on a hamburger
    growing in a garden
    in your blood
    in a movie

19. Where would you find
    a **patella**?
    in a fishing net
    in your body
    in some cookie dough
    on a banana split

20. Where would you find
    a **culprit**?
    in jail
    in a sock drawer
    in casserole

21. Where would you find
    a **lozenge**?
    running in a marathon
    giving hair cuts
    waiting in a medicine
      cabinet
    sunbathing in a lounge
      chair

22. Which of these would
    certainly **NOT be tasty**?
    a query
    a fricassee
    a canapé
    a tempura

23. One of these names a
    bone. Which one?
    contrail
    cliché
    clavicle
    clavichord

24. Which of these would
    you **gnash**?
    your teeth
    your bank account
    cheese
    crystal goblets

25. A **jetty** would probably be
    found near which one?
    a desert
    a bank
    water
    icebergs

Name _____ 105 _____

All the kids were full of **vigor** as they excitedly ran to get the best seats on the roller coaster.

26. In the sentence above, **vigor** means
    a. food   b. energy   c. fear   d. hesitance

Jan's attempt to bungee-jump off the tower was **foiled** by the bad weather.

27. In the sentence above, **foiled** means
    a. prevented   b. helped   c. explained   d. made dangerous

After two hours of waiting in line for *The Twister,* Spike's patience was **waning** and his feet were tired.

28. In the sentence above, **waning** means
    a. growing   b. exploding   c. fading away   d. increasing

"We'll have to go home soon," said Leroy, "since there's a **dearth** of money in our pockets."

29. In the sentence above, **dearth** means
    a. supply   b. loss   c. surplus   d. shortage

Everyone was exhausted after a **grueling** day at the amusement park.

30. In the sentence above, **grueling** means
    a. exciting   b. surprising   c. tiring   d. disappointing

Name _____

Middle Grade Book of Language Tests   Copyright ©2001 by Incentive Publications, Inc., Nashville, TN.

31. Circle the **denotation** of *roller coaster*.

a. a steep, sharply-banked elevated railway with small open passenger cars operated as an attraction at fairgrounds and amusement parks

b. a wild, terrifying amusement park ride that speeds up and down hills, jerking screaming passengers back and forth

32. Circle the **connotation** of *music*.

a. the science of ordering tones

b. wonderful and pleasing rhythmic sounds for dancing

33. Circle the **denotation** of the word *giant*.

a. a huge, frightening, hairy creature that looks strange and threatens people

b. a person or thing of great size and strength

34. Read the **denotation** and **connotation**. Tell what the word is._____

Denotation: a time of day when the sun disappears from sight behind the edge of the horizon

Connotation: beautiful, brilliant colors fill the sky around a golden sun sinking into a blue sea

35. Read the **denotation** and **connotation**. Tell what the word is._____

Denotation: petty and groundless rumors, usually of a personal nature

Connotation: juicy secrets and harmful stories whispered behind someone's back

36. Choose the word below that has the **right connotation** for the sentence.

When Gigi got off the Ferris wheel, she had lost all _____in her arms and legs.

a. consciousness   b. emotion   c. feeling   d. passion

37. Choose the word below that has the **right connotation** for the sentence.

Look at the ____fireworks splattering the sky over the amusement park!

a. elegant   b. handsome   c. spectacular   d. graceful

Middle Grade Book of Language Tests

The line for the *Raging River Rampage* ride was abominable. It was long, slow, and noisy. The family behind us bickered endlessly, and the school kids in front of us were annoyingly boisterous. An arrogant lady pushed her way in front of me, goring me with the huge umbrella she carried. Everyone was impatient; many showed their most boorish behavior. But the ride was worth every minute of the troublesome wait. It began with a relaxing, lethargic float down a sparkling river. After a few minutes, however, the lazy river turned into a wild frothy maelstrom. We were tossed and turned— and sent spinning in repeated circles through thrilling rapids. As we bounced off rocks and plunged over drops, the water washed over us again and again. By the end of the ride, all the churlish waiters-in-line had turned into shrieking, happy river travelers.

Search the story to find a **synonym** for each word below.

_____38. whirlpool

_____39. haughty

_____40. stabbing

_____41. quibbled

_____42. grumpy

Search the story to find an **antonym** for each word below.

_____43. energetic

_____44. polite

_____45. boring

_____46. wonderful

_____47. calm

48. Circle the word that does **NOT** have a similar meaning to the others.

abhor	adore
detest	despise

49. Circle the word that does **NOT** have a similar meaning to the others.

escape	elude
eclipse	evade

50. Circle the word that does **NOT** have a similar meaning to the others.

brawny	brave
burly	husky

51. Circle the word that does **NOT** have a similar meaning to the others.

doleful	gloating
gloomy	somber

Use **context clues** to choose the word that best fits in each sentence below. Circle the word.

52. The wild river ride left us a soaked and _____ with cold.
    jumping   twitching   jerking   shuddering

53. It was a bumpy ride sitting on top of the _____ elephant.
    strolling   lumbering   gliding   sauntering

54. _____ with his friends for leaving him, Leroy was fuming.
    Impatient   Annoyed   Displeased   Furious

55. After being caught in the downpour, our clothes were _____.
    damp   sopping   clammy   muggy

56. The merriment was shattered by a woman's piercing _____.
    roar   bellow   holler   shriek

---

57. Read the different meanings for a word. What is the word? _____

    a. the family and assembly of a king   c. a building surrounded by enclosed grounds

    b. a rectangular space for playing tennis   d. to seek to win a pledge of marriage

---

58. Read the different meanings for a word. What is the word? _____

    a. to follow closely   b. a place to run a race   c. an animal footprint

---

59. Read the different meanings for a word. What is the word? _____

    a. a bone in the human forearm   b. the distance from the center of a circle to its edge

---

60. Write two different meanings for the word *scale*:

    _____

    _____

    Middle Grade Book of Language Tests

CONFUSING WORDS

Name _____

Possible Correct Answers: 55

Date _____

Your Correct Answers: _____

Circle one of the bold words in each question.

1. Four friends take this trip to the amusement park twice a year.
   Is this trip **biennial** or **biannual**?

2. Energetically, Spike raced up the ramp to the *Bigfoot Hall of Fame*.
   Is Spike feeling **vigorous** or **rigorous**?

3. The end of our stay at the amusement park is coming near.
   Is the end of our time here **imminent** or **eminent**?

4. When she rode past the gruesome ghouls in the *Grand Ghastly
   Mansion*, Chichi turned her eyes away from the ghostly scene.
   Did she **avert** her eyes or **invert** her eyes?

5. The girls' favorite ride was closed because a faulty brake needed repair.
   Is the brake **deficient** or **defective**?

6. Chichi screamed at Leroy, "Stop hounding and harassing me to go on this ride!"
   Is Leroy **prosecuting** or **persecuting** Chichi?

7. It took a long time for the operator of *The Terminator* to teach the riders
   how to fasten their safety equipment properly.
   Was the operator **obstructing** or **instructing** the riders?

8. "The *Double-High, Double-Fast, Double-Look, Double-Trouble Roller Coaster* is not dangerous,"
   Leroy promised Spike.
   Did Leroy **assure** or **insure** Spike?

Which word is correct for the meaning of the sentence? Circle the word.

9. Everyone **(accept, except)** Spike has ridden *The Stomach Cruncher* twice.

10. How did that ride **(affect, effect)** your stomach, Leroy?

11. Chichi is extremely **(adept, adopt)** at getting rings around those bottles; she's won three great prizes already!

12. The amusement park manager received several **(complaints, compliments)** that the rides were too short.

13. Did you hear about the guy who took a year off **(collage, college)** to ride a roller coaster for 300 days?

14. Does anybody want to stop and get some **(advice, advise)** from the fortune teller?

15. If you risk going on that ride, I hope you have good health **(assurance, insurance)**!

Which word is correct for the meaning of the sentence? Circle the word.

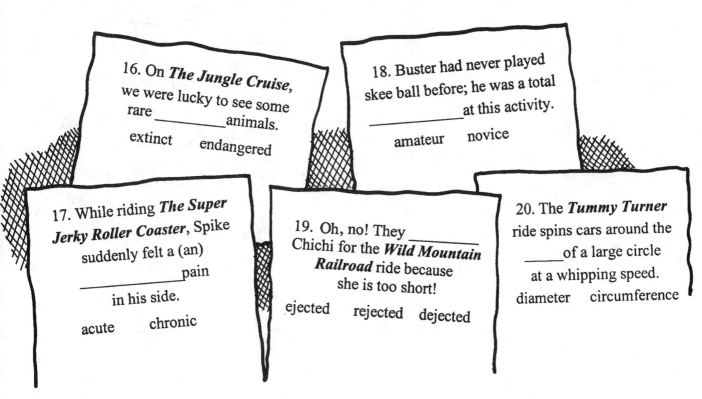

16. On *The Jungle Cruise*, we were lucky to see some rare _____ animals.

extinct   endangered

17. While riding *The Super Jerky Roller Coaster*, Spike suddenly felt a (an) _____ pain in his side.

acute   chronic

18. Buster had never played skee ball before; he was a total _____ at this activity.

amateur   novice

19. Oh, no! They _____ Chichi for the *Wild Mountain Railroad* ride because she is too short!

ejected   rejected   dejected

20. The *Tummy Turner* ride spins cars around the _____ of a large circle at a whipping speed.

diameter   circumference

Name _____

Middle Grade Book of Language Tests

For each word, write a **homonym**—a word that has the same sound, but a different meaning and a different spelling.

21. bawled _____

22. chants _____   27. reign _____

23. sealing _____   28. instants _____

24. quartz _____   29. awed _____

25. cruise _____   30. naval _____

26. heir _____   31. sighs _____

32. FOLLOW ALL THE RULES explained to you buy the assistance who run each ride

33. Stay in you're seat until the safety belt snaps loose and freeze you

34. Anyone cot sneaking on a ride will lose their privilege two use the park

35. KNOW CLIMBING on the tracks of this roller coaster (Violators will be find.)

36. HAVE PATIENTS! The weight for this ride may be long

38. NO MINERS ALOUD in this section (Must be over 18)

39. Had to clothes this ride due to poor whether conditions

37. The fair for this ride is 95 scents

40. Make sure safety belt is tightly rapped around your waste

Each sign above has two words that are **homonyms used incorrectly**. Write the correct homonyms for these signs.

32. _____   35. _____   38. _____

33. _____   36. _____   39. _____

34. _____   37. _____   40. _____

Name _____

Middle Grade Book of Language Tests

Write the letter of the word that matches each history.

_____ 41. from a Greek word meaning *long-haired star*

_____ 42. a Spanish food word meaning a *round, flat cake*

_____ 43. a German food word meaning *sour cabbage*

_____ 44. from New Latin, meaning *eight-footed*

_____ 45. a Portuguese food word meaning *honey*

_____ 46. a Latin food word meaning *head*

_____ 47. an Italian food word meaning *string*

_____ 48. from a Greek word meaning *messenger*

_____ 49. a Russian word meaning *emperor*

a. molasses	g. angel
b. czar	h. cabbage
c. comet	i. piano
d. juvenile	j. spaghetti
e. pajamas	k. tortilla
f. carousel	l. sauerkraut

Circle the correct word for the blank in these **analogies**.

50. **excursion : _____ as physician : doctor**

   excuse   stumble   trip   exercise

51. **jeer : cheer *as* ostracize : _____**

   ostrich   include   reject   prevent

52. **rave : _____ *as* blush : embarrassed**

   whimper   scream   red   angry

53. **_____ : rotten *as* enemy : opponent**

   rancid   fresh   smell   garbage

54. **sprinkles : deluge *as* _____ : blizzard**

   snow   rain   flurries   pour

55. **haughty : humble *as* generous : _____**

   arrogant   selfish   conceited   generosity

STOP

Name _____

Middle Grade Book of Language Tests

Study & Research Skills Checklists

Study & Research Skills Test # 1:

DICTIONARY & ENCYCLOPEDIA SKILLS

Test Location: pages 116–119

Study & Research Skills Test # 2:

REFERENCE & INFORMATION SKILLS

Test Location: pages 120–125

Study & Research Skills Test # 3:

LIBRARY SKILLS

Test Location: pages 126–129

Study & Research Skills Test # 4

STUDY SKILLS

Test Location: pages 130–133

Copyright ©2001 by Incentive Publications, Inc., Nashville, TN.

Middle Grade Book of Language Tests

DICTIONARY & ENCYCLOPEDIA SKILLS

Name _____

Possible Correct Answers: 30

Date _____

Your Correct Answers: _____

1. These detective agencies are listed in the yellow pages. Number them 1–5 in **alphabetical order**.

   _____ Tough Cases To Crack, Inc.

   _____ Travis Tracker Private Eye

   _____ Tucker Detecting, Inc.

   _____ Top Notch Detectives

   _____ Take No Chances Agency

2. Which of the following groups is in **alphabetical order**?

   a. mystery, mystify, mystical, mysticism

   b. mysterious, mystic, mystify, mystique

   c. mystify, mysteries, mystic, mysticism

3. Which of the following groups is in **alphabetical order**?

   a. panic, perform, pharaoh, pizza, prickly

   b. perform, pizza, pharaoh, poorhouse

   c. panic, pizza, poorhouse, plethora

4. Which of the following groups is in **alphabetical order**?

   a. McDonald, McGill, McCarthy, McDowell

   b. McGill, McNamara, MacMillan, McLean

   c. MacDonald, MacMillan, McClure, McGill

5. Number the phrases in **alphabetical order**.

   _____ raining cats and dogs

   _____ chip off the old block

   _____ go out on a limb

   _____ spill the beans

   _____ madder than a wet hen

   _____ cost and arm and a leg

6. Number the titles in **alphabetical order**.

   _____ *The Case of the Invisible President*

   _____ *The Case of the Missing Rap Singer*

   _____ *The Curious Case of the Internet Spies*

   _____ *The Case of the Disappearing Doorknobs*

   _____ *The Challenging Case of Silent Piano*

7. Number the cities in **alphabetical order**.

   _____ Belgium

   _____ Beijing

   _____ Beirut

   _____ Belgrade

   _____ Belfast

   _____ Berkeley

   _____ Bengal

116

Use the dictionary guide words to answer questions 8–10.

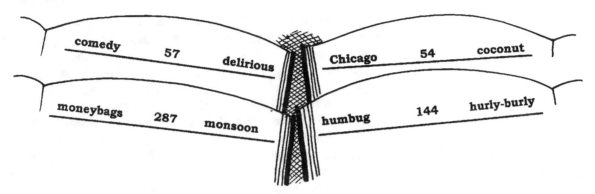

8. Which of the following words would NOT be found on page 54 or 57?

Cinderella   *chicken*   *compost*   *chordates*   *comedian*   *communicable*

9. Which of the following words would be found on page 287?

money order   *monster*   *Monte Carlo*   *monotony*   *monopoly*   *monk*

10. Which of the following words would NOT be found on page 144?

humanoid   *humid*   *hunchback*   *hush-hush*

Use the encyclopedia guide words to answer questions 11–14.

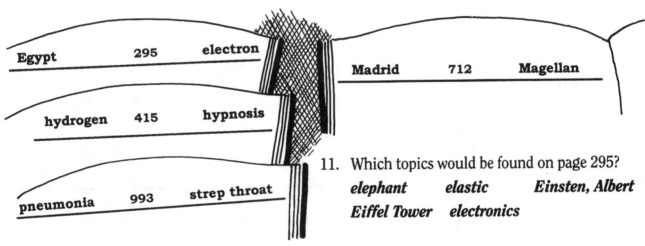

11. Which topics would be found on page 295?

elephant   *elastic*   *Einsten, Albert*
Eiffel Tower   *electronics*

12. Which topics would be found on page 993?

psoriasis   *nausea*   *pink eye*   *tendonitis*   *shingles*

13. Which topics would NOT be found on page 712?

Madison, James   *magnetism*   *mahogany*   *marsupial*   *Madrone*

14. Which topics would NOT be found on page 415?

hydrophobia   *hymns*   *hyena*   *hibernation*   *hysteria*

Middle Grade Book of Language Tests

Great Hall   **gremlins**

green flash a large, deep green, brilliant spark of great intensity that sometimes appears at the final point when the upper edge of the sun disappears below a distant horizon. The green flash is a result of the different degrees to which the components of light are bent (refracted) as white light is broken up (dispersed) by the Earth's atmosphere. When the upper edge of the sun disappears below the horizon, the colors of the white light disappear at different times. Red, orange, and yellow rays disappear first because they are bent the least as they pass through the atmosphere. With only green, indigo, blue, and violet left, the remaining light appears very green. A green flash is best seen over the ocean, but it can be seen over land also. It usually does not happen unless certain conditions exist. The air must be very clear, and the horizon be far away. The flash is usually seen for just a few seconds. However, Admiral Richard E. Byrd, explorer to the Antarctic, claimed to have seen a green flash for 35 minutes on an expedition in 1929.

15. What word in the encyclopedia entry is used to tell that the light rays are bent? _____

16. Which of these conditions need to be present for the green flash to be seen? (Choose one or more.)

   a. The observer must be looking at the sky over the ocean.

   b. The air is especially clear.

   c. The horizon is distant.

   d. The sunset must be red, orange, and yellow.

   e. The upper edge of the sun is at the point of disappearing below the horizon.

   f. The observer must be in Antarctica.

Which is the **best key word or phrase** for an encyclopedia search for each of the topics?

17. the cause of static electricity

energy   static

electric   lightning

19. how the body fights germs

blood cells   human body

diseases   germs

18. the story of the sinking of the *Titanic*

ships   shipwrecks   icebergs

ocean travel   Arctic Ocean   *Titanic*

20. the height of the Eiffel Tower

Paris   landmarks   Eiffel

buildings   towers   history

Name _____

Middle Grade Book of Language Tests

pedestal \'ped-əs-tl\ *n* the base of an upright structure

personally \'pərs-nə-lē\ *adv* in person

peruse \pə-'rūz\ *v* to examine or consider in detail

pervasive \pər-'vā-siv\ *adj* that goes throughout

pesky \'pes-kē\ *adj* troublesome

peso \' pā-sō\ *n pl* pesos [*Sp.* weight] an old silver coin of Spain and Spanish America

pessimism \'pəs-ə-miz-əm\ *n* a tendency to emphasize adverse aspects, conditions, or possibilities, or expect the worse

pester \'pes-tər\ *v* pes-tered; pes-ter-ing \ to harass

pestilence \'pes-tə-ləns\ *n* 1. a devastating, contagious, infectious disease 2. something that is destructive

1**pestle** \'pes-təl\ *n* a club-shaped instrument used for grinding substances in a mortar

2**pestle** \'pes-təl\ *v* to beat, pound, or pulverize with a pestle

pesto \'pes-tō\ *n* [*It., Fr.* pounded] a sauce made of ingredients pounded or pressed together, especially garlic, oil, pine nuts, and cheese

petite \pə-'tēt\ *adj* [*Fr.* small] having a small trim figure

petit fours \pet-e-'fõrz\ *n* [*Fr.* small oven] a small cake cut from pound or sponge cake and frosted

1**petition** \pə-'tish-ən\ *n* 1. a strong request 2. a document making a formal written request

2**petition** \pə-'tish-ən\ *v* to make an urgent request

pet napping \'pet-nap-ing\ *n* the act of stealing a pet, usually for profit

pet peeve \pet 'pēv\ *n* a frequent subject of complaint

petrify \'pe-trə-fī\ *v* 1. to convert into stone or a stony substance 2. to make rigid or lifeless 3. to frighten

21. Which word or words are adverbs? _____

22. Which words are adjectives? _____

23. Which words are both nouns and verbs? _____

24. Which words are shown with two or more meanings? _____

25. From which language is *petit fours* borrowed? _____

26. Which words name things that can be eaten? _____

27. Which word means *a subject of complaint*? _____

28. Which word is an antonym for *optimism*? _____

29. Which word is a synonym for *bother*? _____

30. Which word means *a disease*? _____

Name _____

Middle Grade Book of Language Tests

REFERENCE & INFORMATION SKILLS

Name _____   Possible Correct Answers: 75

Date _____   Your Correct Answers: _____

Match the names of each reference book on the detective's notepad with the correct description. Write the number of the description on the line before the correct book name.

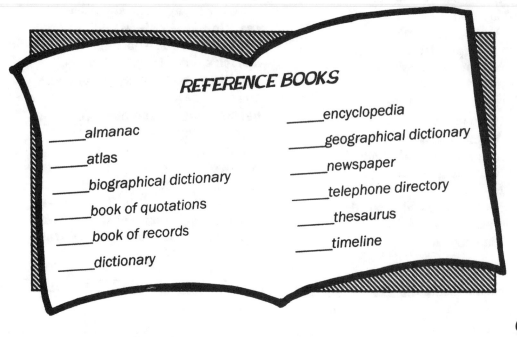

REFERENCE BOOKS

_____almanac

_____atlas

_____biographical dictionary

_____book of quotations

_____book of records

_____dictionary

_____encyclopedia

_____geographical dictionary

_____newspaper

_____telephone directory

_____thesaurus

_____timeline

1. a collection of words and their synonyms
2. a collection of maps bound into a book
3. a book of interesting or important statements that have been made
4. a collection of words arranged alphabetically, that gives information about the words' meanings, uses, forms, pronunciations, and histories
5. a collection of information in one or more volumes on many subjects, gathered together in articles that are alphabetically arranged
6. a collection of articles telling about the lives of people and their accomplishments, arranged alphabetically
7. a sequential list of events represented by a diagram and arranged by dates
8. a book that is published yearly, containing a variety of general and numerical information
9. a book of current records of sporting events and various other events and accomplishments
10. an alphabetical listing of the names of places in the world and their descriptions and locations

Which reference should you use to find each of the following kinds of information?
Choose the best reference for each task from the detective's list.
Write the letter of the reference on the line.

A. atlas

B. almanac

C. biographical dictionary

D. dictionary

E. encyclopedia

F. encyclopedia index

G. geographical dictionary

H. Guinness Book of Records

I. index of quotations

J. Internet

K. library catalog

L. newspaper

M. quotation index

N. telephone directory

O. thesaurus

_____11. if this word is spelled correctly: *ambidexterous*

_____12. a history of the word *carousel*

_____13. the first woman to climb Mt. Everest

_____14. five words that mean the same as *mystery*

_____15. the location of China's largest cities

_____16. the title of a book of poetry by John Ciardi

_____17. the history of the abominable snowman

_____18. who said, "Give me liberty or give me death!"

_____19. a list of exterminators in your area

_____20. the correct pronunciation of the word *petit fours*

_____21. the author of the book, *Never Eat Peanuts in Church*

_____22. the present population of Alabama

_____23. the climate of Malaysia

_____24. products produced in Turkey

_____25. a weather forecast for tomorrow in your city

_____26. a short biography of Eleanor Roosevelt

_____27. the cost of a book about Harry Potter

_____28. an antonym for the word *obnoxious*

_____29. a good hotel in Bangkok, Thailand

_____30. the latest Olympic Gold medalist in men's figure skating

_____31. a weather forecast for tomorrow in Budapest, Hungary

_____32. the titles of some books by the author, Nathaniel Hawthorne

_____33. the name of the current record holder for bathtub racing

_____34. which encyclopedia volumes give information about global warming

Name _____

121

Match the words on the left with their definitions.

a. *index*

b. *table of contents*

c. *cover*

d. *title page*

e. *glossary*

f. *copyright page*

_____ 35. a list of terms used in the book, along with their definitions

_____ 36. the outside of a book; contains title and author

_____ 37. a page near the front of the book; contains the name of the publisher and copyright date

_____ 38. the first page of the book; contains the title, author, and publisher

_____ 39. an alphabetical list of topics in a book and their page numbers

_____ 40. a list of sections in the book and their page numbers, arranged in the order they occur in the book

Table of Contents

Use the Table of Contents to answer questions 41–47.

41. In which chapters would you find cases involving animals? _____

42. What pages cover break-ins and burglaries? _____

43. Which chapter is the longest? _____

44. Which pages cover a factory break-in?

_____

45. On what page can you begin reading about a case that involves money? _____

46. Which chapters have cases that involve food? _____

47. How many pages cover the disappearances?

_____

Name _____

Middle Grade Book of Language Tests   Copyright ©2001 by Incentive Publications, Inc., Nashville, TN.

Use the Index for questions 48–54.

INDEX

48. On what pages can you read about a robbery? _____

49. Where will you find the Scents Over the Internet case? _____

50. What pages tell about the Safety-Pin Factory robbery? _____

51. Where can you read about skydiving mice? _____

52. Which pages cover strange occurrences? _____

53. Which pages cover burglaries? _____

54. On what pages can you read about disappearances? _____

Use the illustration above for questions 55–56.

55. From what the pictures shows, which of these statements are (is) probably true? (Circle the letters.)

    a. The picture was hanging over the safe.

    b. The safe has been robbed.

    c. The intruder was in a hurry.

    d. Someone got hit with a lamp.

56. From what the picture shows, which of these statements are (is) probably true? (Circle the letters.)

    a. The window was broken from the outside.

    b. The window was broken from the inside.

    c. The person who made the footprints came from the outside.

    d. The break-in happened just before the picture was taken.

Name _____

Middle Grade Book of Language Tests

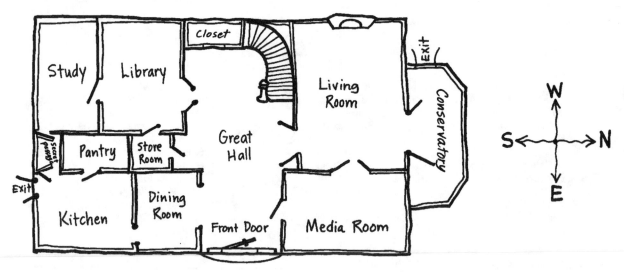

Use this map for questions 57–60.

57. Which room is the furthest north in the house?
   a. media room
   b. living room
   c. kitchen
   d. conservatory

58. Which is NOT further west than the dining room?
   a. study
   b. pantry
   c. media room
   d. closet

59. Which direction does the front door face? _____

60. Is there a route that could be taken from the study to the media room which would pass through 5 rooms (not counting the media room and study)?

   _____

Use the timeline for questions 61-66.

Timeline (Jan–Dec):
- Missing Prom Queen (Jan)
- Safety-Pin Robbery (Feb)
- Anonymous Money Drop (Apr)
- Mysterious Scents (May)
- Missing City Hall (Jun)
- Ant Farm Break-In (Jul)
- The Missing Doughnut Holes (Aug/Sept)
- Yogurt Robbery (Sept)
- Skydiving Mice (Oct)
- Missing DVD Player (Nov)
- Missing Basketball Nets (Dec)

61. About how many months passed between robberies? _____

62. What was missing about 4 months before the basketball nets? _____

63. What case took place about 4 ½ months after the anonymous money drop? _____

64. Which cases took place during April? _____

65. During which months did the detective have no challenging cases? _____

66. About how many months passed between cases involving animals? _____

Use the table below for questions 67–70.

Case Type	J. Jolly	S. Snoop	U. Surch	I.V. Looky	S. Wiley
CASE ASSIGNMENTS					
Robberies	41	3	7	13	6
Missing Persons	7	4	9	2	6
Missing Animals	12	31	20	17	37
Assaults	6	12	16	22	19
Suspicious Noises	4	18	29	42	40

67. The greatest number of cases were of what type? _____

68. How many detectives investigated more assaults than robberies? _____

69. How many detectives had more cases of suspicious noises than any other case type? _____

70. How many more cases were assigned to S. Wiley than S. Snoop? _____

Use the graph below for questions 71–75.

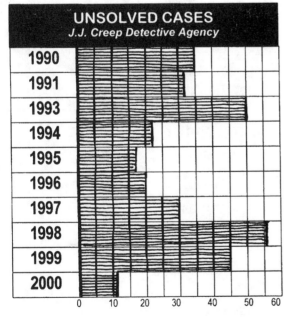

71. Which year had 32 unsolved cases? _____

72. Which year had 30 fewer unsolved cases than 1993? _____

73. About how many more cases were unsolved in 1994 than 2000? _____

74. During what 4-year period were the fewest cases left unsolved? _____

75. About how many cases were unsolved in 1998? _____

Middle Grade Book of Language Tests

LIBRARY SKILLS

Name _____   Possible Correct Answers: 50

Date _____   Your Correct Answers: _____

1. This book is probably:
   a. fiction
   b. nonfiction
   c. biography

2. This book is probably:
   a. fiction
   b. nonfiction
   c. biography

3. This book is probably:
   a. fiction
   b. nonfiction
   c. biography

4. Biographies are organized:
   a. alphabetically by author
   b. alphabetically by title
   c. alphabetically by the person
   d. alphabetically by subject

5. Fiction is organized:
   a. alphabetically by author
   b. alphabetically by title
   c. by the Dewey Decimal System
   d. alphabetically by subject

6. If you know the subject of a book, but not the author or title, you could find the book by looking at the:
   a. subject card
   b. author card
   c. title card

7. To find a mystery written by Anne Perry, which word would you type into the library computer catalog?
   a. Anne
   b. Perry
   c. mysteries
   d. fiction

Middle Grade Book of Language Tests   Copyright ©2001 by Incentive Publications, Inc., Nashville, TN.

796
Ja   **SPORTS--ANECDOTES**
        Jameson, Andrea
        Hilarious Sports Blunders
        Illust. by Damon Ryan
      Chicago: C. Sports, Inc: © 1975
        324 p. illus.

PE1689.F76   **FUNK, CHARLES EARLE**
        A Hog on Ice
        Illust. by Tom Funk
       NY: Harper & Row
          © 1948
        214 p. illus.

8. What kind of a card is this?
    a. author b. subject c. title

9. Who is the publisher?

_____

10. Is the book illustrated? _____

11. What is the title?

_____

17. What kind of a card is this?
    a. author b. subject c. title

18. Where was the book published?

_____

19. What is the title? _____

20. Who is the illustrator?

_____

Fic   **ALIENS--STORIES**
Mol   Molhalland, Hugh
      Strange Sights in the Night Sky
        Illust. by Julia Lynton
      Omaha: Night Sky Press © 1999
        244 p. illus.

Fic   Lost in Deep Space
Tao   Tappan, Zoie
          Illust. by Aubrey Wrapp
       NY: Universe © 1988
        160 p. illus.

12. Who is the author?

_____

13. What is the title?

_____

14. What is the copyright date? _____

15. Who is the illustrator?

_____

16. How many pages are in the book?

_____

21. What kind of card is this?
    a. author b. subject c. title

22. Who is the illustrator?

_____

23. What is the title? _____

24. What is the copyright date? _____

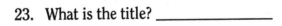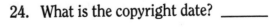

Name _____

Middle Grade Book of Language Tests

In which section of the library would each of these books be found?
Write the Dewey Decimal System section.
(For example, write *100*.)

100-199	Philosophy & Psychology
200-299	Religion & Myths
300-399	Social Sciences
400-499	Languages
500-599	Natural Science & Math
600-699	Uses of Science & Technology
700-799	Fine Arts & Sports
800-899	Literature
900-999	History, Geography, Biography

_____ 25. *Learn to Speak Japanese*

_____ 26. *Poems to Make Your Friends Laugh*

_____ 27. *Understanding the Behavior of Teenagers*

_____ 28. *200 Hilarious Airplane Jokes*

_____ 29. *The A-B-Cs of Biology*

_____ 30. *Different Faiths for Different Folks*

_____ 31. *You Could Be a Great Actor*

_____ 32. *Guide to the World's Highest Mountains*

_____ 33. *The Life Story of Detective C. McGee*

_____ 34. *Mastering Those Tricky Ice-Skating Jumps*

_____ 35. *Algebra for Math-o-Phobics*

_____ 36. *Myths of Africa*

_____ 37. *The History of Snowboarding*

_____ 38. *200 Cool Things for Kids to Do on the Internet*

_____ 39. *Curious Facts about World Cultures*

_____ 40. *Yes, Even You Can Learn to Ballet Dance*

Name _____

Middle Grade Book of Language Tests

41. Number these fiction books in the order in which they would appear on a library shelf.

☐ *The Mysterious Disappearance of the English Channel*
by Audrey M. Credible

☐ ***Buster's Afternoon in a Wormhole***
by J.J. Cadet

☐ **NEVER SAY HELLO TO BIGFOOT**
by Esther Goner

☐ **The Strange Occurrence at South Park High**
by Seymour Principle

☐ *The Day My Backpack Turned into Jello*
by Elmer J. Jiggle

☐ *The Detective Who Couldn't Detect a Thing*
by Ima Pringle

Write a letter to match each Internet term
with its correct description.

a. cookies	h. HTML
b. browser	i. surfing
c. server	j. user ID
d. modem	k. graphics
e. search engine	l. SPAM
f. download	m. com
g. home page	n. URL

_____ 42. bits of text that a Web site leaves on your computer for tracking information about your preferences

_____ 43. a program designed to explore the Internet to look for specific information

_____ 44. annoying, unwanted Internet mail

_____ 45. to transfer data to the user's computer from another computer

_____ 46. the name you use to identify yourself to your on-line service

_____ 47. a software tool that lets you visit sites on the World Wide Web

_____ 48. a computer or system that provides access to the Internet

_____ 49. the starting page of a World Wide Web site

_____ 50. an address for a source on the World Wide Web

Name _____

Middle Grade Book of Language Tests

STUDY SKILLS

Name _____

Possible Correct Answers: 15

Date _____

Your Correct Answers: _____

CASE # 1

Detective Sam Snoop received a call at 8:00 a.m. from the high school principal. Principal Parker reported that all the basketball nets had disappeared from both gymnasiums. The extra nets, kept in the storage rooms, had disappeared as well. School officials were baffled by this, and had no ideas about what might have happened. Detective Snoop grabbed his notebook, pen, and looking glass, and headed for the high school.

CASE # 2

Something strange has been occurring in Pleasant City. Someone has been breaking into homes all over town. Nothing has been reported stolen. What is strange is that, in each case, the bathtub was found full of warm water and bubbles. Wet, soapy footprints and damp towels have also been found at each scene. Twelve similar reports were filed this week. This, added to previous reports, brings the total of incidents involving a "serial bather" to thirty-four. So far, police have found no clues to the identity of the bather.

Read Case #1.

1. Circle the questions that could help Detective Snoop learn important information that may help him figure out what happened to the nets.
   a. When did you notice the disappearance?
   b. Who told you about the disappearance?
   c. How many nets were there?
   d. Who has access to the gymnasiums?
   e. When were the nets last seen in place?
   f. Who has access to the storage rooms?
   g. Who knew the location of the extra nets?
   h. How old were the nets?
   i. When is the next game scheduled?
   j. Were the doors to the rooms unlocked?

Skim Case #2 quickly. Without looking back through the story, answer these questions.

2. How did the suspect gain access to the homes? _____

3. How many incidents of serial bathing were reported this week? _____

4. Which of these clues was NOT left behind?
   damp towels   warm bath water
   bathtub toys   wet footprints

Middle Grade Book of Language Tests

Copyright ©2001 by Incentive Publications, Inc., Nashville, TN.

CASE # 3

An urgent call came in to the *We-Solve-It Detective Agency* at 6:30 p.m. "My business is ruined!" screamed the agitated restaurant owner. "Help! Mice! There are mice everywhere! They are falling from the sky!"

Detective Cici Sharp calmed the agitated restaurant owner to get the story. This is what the detective was told. Just at the height of the busy dinner hour at the elegant *Les Manages* restaurant, dozens of mice floated down from the sky, wearing tiny parachutes. The mice landed on the outdoor dining patio of the restaurant, and began racing around the floor and across the tables.

According to Patrice, the owner, the restaurant is located next to a pet shop. He recently filed a suit against the pet shop owner because the odors from the shop were detrimental to his business, he claimed. Patrice described the mouse incident: "They just came out of nowhere. We heard no airplane. We saw nothing else in the sky. I was just serving cream of leek soup to a large group of guests. All of a sudden, a hundred tiny red parachutes were overhead. We heard loud squeaking, and then they landed. One mouse landed in a customer's soup. The mice started eating the salads. The parachutes were tied onto the mice with red shoelaces. They were so disgusting. All my guests ran away screaming. What shall I do? No one will ever come back to my restaurant!"

5. What is the main idea of the case?

_____

6. Which details are relevant to the case? (Which details would be likely to give the detective information that would help solve the case?) Circle all that are necessary.

a. There was no plane or anything else seen in the sky.

b. A law suit had been filed against the pet shop.

c. The incident happened at the busy dinner hour.

d. The parachutes were tied with red shoelaces.

e. The restaurant owner was agitated.

f. There is a pet shop next door.

g. There were dozens of mice.

h. The mice were wearing parachutes.

i. The leek soup had just been served.

j. The mice ate the salads.

     Middle Grade Book of Language Tests

CASE # 4

The first call about the strange Internet scents came into the agency at midnight on Friday. Dozens of people wanted an immediate investigation. It seems that, every time users logged on to the Internet, using the new Sweet Surfing browser, smells began emanating from the monitors of their computers. People have reported a variety of smells, pleasant and unpleasant. Callers have described the following smells: skunk, fried onions, citrus, wet dog, locker room, lilies, pizza, coffee, and gingerbread. Detective Scan, an Internet specialist, has been assigned to the case.

7. Which is the best summary of Case #4?

   a. A new browser causes bad smells.

   b. Strange scents are coming over the Internet.

   c. Internet users are looking for an investigator.

Read each brief news article below. Write a headline that accurately summarizes the main idea of each article.

8. *Morning News, July 4, 1999*

_____

_____

A curious occurrence has been happening all over the city. Bundles of money are turning up in trash cans in city parks. No one has been seen leaving the money. There have been forty reports of such incidents. The bundles contain amounts of money up to $5000.

9. *The Gazette, September 4, 1998*

_____

_____

Yesterday at noon, citizens who were on their way to do business at City Hall were in for a shock. At precisely noon, City Hall disappeared. The entire building just vanished. At midnight, the building was back in place. The FBI is on the scene to investigate. The National Guard is standing by.

10. *Daily Tidings, Saturday, April 3, 2000*

_____

_____

A gigantic ant farm disappeared last night from the city zoo. The farm, contained in a glass case weighing 800 pounds, holds about 10,000 biting red ants. Citizens are requested to report any information they might have about the missing ant farm.

Name _____

Middle Grade Book of Language Tests

Write the numbers or letters showing where each of these missing pieces belongs in the outline. (Example: write II A.)

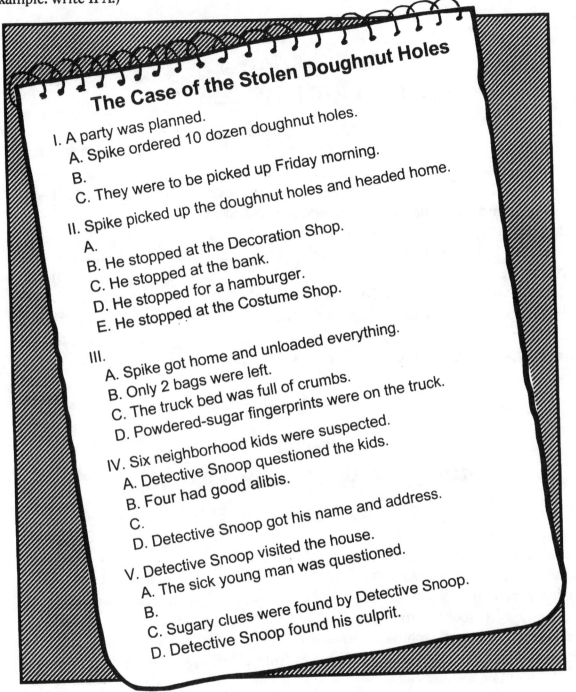

The Case of the Stolen Doughnut Holes

I. A party was planned.
   A. Spike ordered 10 dozen doughnut holes.
   B.
   C. They were to be picked up Friday morning.

II. Spike picked up the doughnut holes and headed home.
   A.
   B. He stopped at the Decoration Shop.
   C. He stopped at the bank.
   D. He stopped for a hamburger.
   E. He stopped at the Costume Shop.

III.
   A. Spike got home and unloaded everything.
   B. Only 2 bags were left.
   C. The truck bed was full of crumbs.
   D. Powdered-sugar fingerprints were on the truck.

IV. Six neighborhood kids were suspected.
   A. Detective Snoop questioned the kids.
   B. Four had good alibis.
   C.
   D. Detective Snoop got his name and address.

V. Detective Snoop visited the house.
   A. The sick young man was questioned.
   B.
   C. Sugary clues were found by Detective Snoop.
   D. Detective Snoop found his culprit.

_____ 11. They were ordered from Pete's Bakery.

_____ 12. The young man's fingerprints were taken.

_____ 13. One was sick in bed with a stomachache.

_____ 14. Eight bags were discovered missing.

_____ 15. He put the 10 bags in his truck.

Name _____ **133** _____

Spelling Skills Checklists

Spelling Skills Test # 1:

RULES & RULE BREAKERS

Test Location: pages 136–139

Skill	*Test Items*
Correctly spell words that use *ie* rules	1–15
Correctly spell words that follow rules for adding endings and suffixes	16–22
Spell words with confusing tricky consonant sounds and blends	23–34
Follow rules to spell plurals correctly	35–42
Correctly spell the singular form of a plural noun	43–50
Correctly spell words with double consonants	51–56
Follow rules to correctly spell different tenses of verbs	57–59
Correctly spell the past tense of irregular verbs	60–65
Correctly spell a variety of compound words	66–74
Correctly spell words that break spelling rules	75–84

Spelling Skills Test # 2:

SPELLING WITH WORD PARTS

Test Location: pages 140–143

Skill	*Test Items*
Correctly spell words with prefixes	1–10, 21–30
Correctly spell words with suffixes	11–20, 21–30
Correctly spell words that have a prefix and a suffix	21–30
Use knowledge of root spellings to spell words correctly	31–44
Make correct changes to root words when adding *ed* or *ing*	45–52
Distinguish among similar endings; choose the correct ending for accurate spelling	53–70

Spelling Skills Test # 3:

CONFUSING & TRICKY WORDS

Test Location: pages 144–147

Skill	*Test Items*
Identify correctly and incorrectly spelled words containing silent letters	1
Correctly spell words of foreign origin	2–8
Correctly spell words with special vowel combinations	9–24
Spell and distinguish between words that look or sound similar	25–33
Correctly spell big words	34–37
Correctly spell a variety of confusing words	38–50

Spelling Skills Test # 4:

CORRECTING SPELLING ERRORS

Test Location: pages 148–152

Skill	*Test Items*
Correct spelling errors in proper nouns	1–12
Correct errors in titles or headlines	13–18
Correct errors in food words	19–27
Find and correct misspelled words in phrases	28–44
Find and correct misspelled words in short passages	45–50
Find and correct misspelled words on signs	51–58
Correct misspelled words within sentences	59–66
Correct misspelled words in a letter and on an envelope	67–85

RULES & RULE BREAKERS

Name _____

Date _____

Possible Correct Answers: 84

Your Correct Answers: _____

Circle the **correct spelling** for each word.

1. freind friend	**2.** achieve acheive	**3.** believe beleive	**4.** deciet deceit
5. retreive retrieve	**6.** sleigh sliegh	**7.** grief greif	**8.** nieghbor neighbor
9. deceive decieve	**10.** concieted conceited	**11.** frieght freight	**12.** percieve perceive
13. cieling ceiling	**14.** reciept receipt	**15.** vien vein	

Each of these words is spelled incorrectly. Follow spelling rules to **write them correctly**.

16. sincerly_____

17. shiney _____

18. fameous_____

19. marryiage _____

20. hotest _____

21. shoping_____

22. busynes_____

Leroy is writing some clever phrases. One word in each phrase is spelled **incorrectly**. Circle the word.

23. Whose king is in the most greivus danger?
24. Have you seen a ghost in the getto?
25. The faraoh has pneumonia.
26. Is the jiant covered with jelly?
27. That gnome is noisily nashing his teeth!
28. Feed the rubarb to the scholar.
29. A knaughty knight tied knots.
30. Which physician likes fysics?
31. Can you write a psalm that rymes?
32. Could a chromosome play a zylophone?
33. Don't ever give sider to a centipede.
34. Who cut the chorus's music with a sissors?

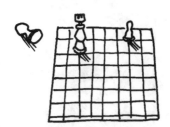

Write each noun in its **plural form**.		Write each noun in its **singular form**.	
35. one rodeo	two _____	43. three mice	one_____
36. one fox	three_____	44. six zeroes	one_____
37. one mosquito	ten_____	45. three loaves	one_____
38. one donkey	five _____	46. five geniuses	one_____
39. one brother-in-law	four_____	47. ten tomatoes	one_____
40. one tooth	fifteen_____	48. nine cities	one_____
41. one holiday	three _____	49. eight haloes	one_____
42. one dragonfly	twenty_____	50. two geese	one_____

Name _____

Middle Grade Book of Language Tests

Look for the words that are spelled **incorrectly**.
Write each of those words correctly on one of the lines.

horrid *balott*

51._____ 52._____

embarassed *marshmallow*

53._____ 54._____

butterscotch

omitted *messenger* *anniversary*

55._____

parralell *cellophane* *bizzarre*

56._____ *oppossum* *barracuda* *squabble*

catterpillar

57. Which sentence shows correct spelling for all the verb tenses?

A. Skydivers droped from the plane like falling people-packages.

B. We hurried to watch the divers leaping from the circling planes.

C. "Is the parachute opening?" cryed the skydiver's sister.

58. Which sentence shows correct spelling for all the verb tenses?

A. She has written three best-selling books on skydiving.

B. How many contests were won before retireing from diveing?

C. After you've jumped, are you freezeing up there in the air?

59. Which sentence shows correct spelling for all the verb tenses?

A. She asked how I liked competeing in skydiving contests.

B. I tolled her that it happens to be the most exciting feeling in the world.

C. "What about the time you crashed into a tree?" she asked.

Write the past tense of each verb.

60. freeze _____ 63. shine _____

61. catch _____ 64. sleep _____

62. fry _____ 65. bring _____

Circle the **incorrectly-spelled** compound word in each group.

66. bookkeeper notebook bubblgum	67. folktale roomate nighttime	68. hitchiker pastime rainmaker
69. candlestick horsfly fireside	70. downtown underwear headdache	71. sholace seashell afternoon
72. sunburn baskettball horseshoe	73. knockout lighthouse homwork	74. sunstroke fircracker quicksand

Choose the **correct spelling** for each word.

75. ancient
    anceint

76. counterfiet
    counterfeit

77. caffeine
    caffiene

78. wholly
    wholey

79. couragous
    courageous

80. financeir
    financier

81. pastime
    pasttime

82. truly
    truley

83. altos
    altoes

84. forfeit
    forfiet

Name _____ **139** _____

SPELLING WITH WORD PARTS

Name _____   Possible Correct Answers: 70

Date _____   Your Correct Answers: _____

All the words on Leroy's test have prefixes or suffixes. Which ones has he spelled correctly?
Find the correct words. Circle their numbers.
Find the incorrect words. Fix the errors by writing the words correctly.

SPELLING TEST

1. subnormal _____

2. postpone _____

3. displace _____

4. multitalented _____

5. innterstate _____

6. antebacterial _____

7. equidistant _____

8. minivan _____

9. preview _____

10. extraordinary _____

11. energise _____

12. spherical _____

13. hardship _____

14. acter _____

15. horrifick _____

16. treacherus _____

17. infantile _____

18. hopful _____

19. wooden _____

20. circuler _____

21. disectioun _____

22. micrascopic _____

23. irreversible _____

24. unresponsave _____

25. entanglement _____

26. forseeable _____

27. distastefull _____

28. unfriendliness _____

29. impossibility _____

30. disagreeible _____

Which word in each sentence is **NOT spelled correctly**? Circle the word.

31. The dentist plays great music while he does ekxtractions of teeth.

32. The condition of this tooth is unbeleivably bad.

33. I'm sorry that your tooth is unstabel, and I'll have to remove it.

34. No, your inshurance is not going to cover this dental work.

35. Let's have a descussion about your poor care of your teeth.

Use your knowledge of roots to **spell these words correctly.** They all have errors.

36. disapear   _____

37. surprizing   _____

38. diference   _____

39. faverable   _____

40. accadental   _____

41. trubblesome   _____

42. invizible   _____

43. freqwently   _____

44. reflecktion   _____

Add **ed** or **ing** to the word at the end of each sentence to make it fit correctly.
Write the word in the blank. Make sure you spell it right!

45. Spike has been _____ all week to avoid a trip to the doctor. (hope)

46. Finally, he _____ up the courage to keep his appointment. (work)

47. As he sat in the waiting room, he _____ his knuckles. (crack)

48. Spike was so _____ about what the doctor would find. (worry)

49. The nurse _____ him to come for an x-ray. (call)

50. "Oh, my," the nurse _____ as she looked at the x-ray. (mumble)

51. Spike _____ a happy tune to keep from being nervous. (hum)

52. He _____ hard when he heard the word *surgery*. (swallow)

Which ending gives the correct spelling to each word?
Circle the correctly-spelled word.

53.	56.	59.
advantege	dangerus	occasion
advantage	dangereous	occashun
advantige	dangerious	occasioun
advantedge	dangerous	occasun
54.	**57.**	**60.**
knowledge	insurince	vessil
knowlege	insurance	vessle
knowlidge	insurence	vessel
knowlage	insurense	vessal
55.	**58.**	**61.**
criticise	prevenshun	fragel
criticize	preventioun	fragal
critisise	preventun	fragile
critisice	prevention	fragil

Circle all the **correctly-spelled** words in each group.

62.
selfish
cowardice
punitive
burglarise
varnesh
realist

63.
optimizm
favoritizm
juvenile
favorate
accurite
florist

64.
abolish
apologise
negativ
exercise
infantile
fragile

65.
nuisance
absence
negligense
consequense
presence

66.
dangerous
couragous
rigorus
marvelous
feroceous
cactis
circus
focus
vicious

67.
obstacel
radical
practicle
traval
quarrel
candel
brutal

68.
dependent
redundent
observint
important
elegant
migrant
distent

69.
prevention
occasion
traditon
magicion
fortune
decision
vacation

70.
impossible
reversible
noticeable
ventricle
practicel
level
rural

CONFUSING & TRICKY WORDS

Name _____   Possible Correct Answers: 50

Date _____   Your Correct Answers: _____

1. Which words in Chichi's dream are spelled **incorrectly**? Circle them.

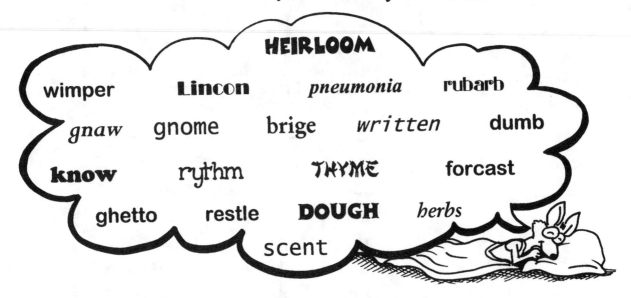

These clues will suggest a word that has been borrowed from a foreign language.
Write the word to match each clue. Spell the word correctly.

2. long, Italian stringy pasta that's served with sauce   **S**_____

3. pesky insect that buzzes, bites, and leaves you itchy   **M**_____

4. the grade in school before first grade   **K**_____

5. a round breakfast pastry with a hole in the middle   **D**_____

6. a sparkling, white gem-stone of great value   **D**_____

7. the driver of a limousine   **CH**_____

8. a merry-go-round   **C**_____

Choose the **right vowel combination** from the chart to spell each word correctly.

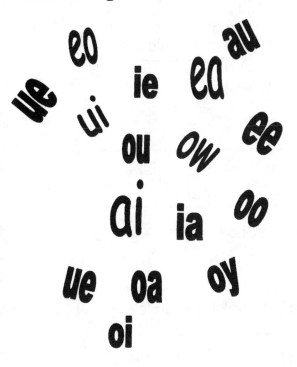

9. l_____pard *(a large cat with spots)*

10. tr_____cherous *(dangerous)*

11. p_____per *(someone very poor)*

12. infl_____nza *(a sickness, usually a virus)*

13. turqu_____se *(a bluish-green color)*

14. disg_____se *(to hide or change identity)*

15. b_____rd *(facial hair)*

16. dr_____ght *(lack of water for a long time)*

Circle the word from each group that is **spelled correctly**.

17.	18.	19.	20.
hygeen	thesaurous	terrane	camoflage
hygiene	thesarus	terriane	camouflage
hygeine	thesourus	terrain	camaugflage
hygene	thesaurus	teraine	camouflag

21. Which words are spelled correctly? Circle them.

   unique   fraud   plausible   hier

22. Which words are spelled correctly? Circle them.

   hoarse   chaos   elouquent   officeal

23. Which words are spelled correctly? Circle them.

   cauliflower   Eisenhower   bouysterous   dinosaur

24. Which words are spelled correctly? Circle them.

   bias   refrane   cooger   resturant

Name _____   145

Circle **yes** or **no** to answer questions 25–27.

> Our new cereal has chunks of tuna fish and marshmallow in it.

25. Is the word **cereal** used (and spelled) correctly for the sentence?   **yes**   **no**

> I have three poems about garbage that will be published
> in the next addition of the school paper.

26. Is the word **addition** used (and spelled) correctly for the sentence?   **yes**   **no**

> Did you get the good meat out of the crab's clause?

27. Is the word **clause** used (and spelled) correctly for the sentence?   **yes**   **no**

Circle the word that **correctly finishes** each sentence.

28. When he explored the *Caves of Confusion*, Spike ran straight into a
(stalactite, stalagmite) hanging from the ceiling of the cave.

29. It happened because he was having a hard time **(adopting, adapting)**
to his new glasses.

30. "It's a bad bump, Spike," said Rufus, "but don't scream and get
(historical, hysterical) about it!"

31. It's too bad Spike forgot to pay for his **(assurance, insurance)** policy!

32. When he came out of the cave, his friends teased him and gave him
(compliments, complaints) on the beautiful bruise on his forehead.

33. "Your teasing is **(all together, altogether)** unacceptable," Spike shouted.

In each sentence below, one big word is spelled wrong.

Find it and **write it correctly** near the sentence.

34. The talented painter from Albaquerquey is ambidextrous.

35. Surprisingly, the extraterrestrial visitors showed very few pecularities.

36. Does your exceptional friend from the symphonic orchestra play a susaphone?

37. The geologist, the psyciatrist, and the pharmacist were all passengers on that ship.

Find the misspelled word in each phrase. Write the word correctly on the line.

38. an outrageous tatoo _____

39. a surprisingly beautiful anenome _____

40. music with stacato rhythm _____

41. a most bizarre set of sircumstances _____

42. an inconvenient, untimely catastrophy _____

43. an expensive cordaroy athletic jacket _____

Circle the **incorrect word** in each group.

44. karate	breakable	suspiscious	impossible
45. opponent	absourb	torpedoes	omitted
46. vehicle	protien	embarrass	interrupt
47. noticable	macaroni	lozenge	peculiar
48. amatur	conscience	ceremony	extravagant
49. sheik	immingrant	ammonia	recognition
50. Tennessee	Mississippi	Flordia	Illinois

Middle Grade Book of Language Tests

CORRECTING SPELLING ERRORS

Name _____

Date _____

Possible Correct Answers: 85

Your Correct Answers: _____

This poor speller is having a terrible time with proper nouns.
Find the misspelled words. **Spell them correctly** on the lines below.

1. Brooklyn Bridge, United Natians _____

2. Atlantic, Pacific, Carribbean _____

3. Lincoln, Eisenhouer, Washington _____

4. Chacago, Miami, Tallahassee _____

5. Christmas, Haloween, Thanksgiving _____

6. Cambodia, Belguim, Ecuador _____

7. Missourri, Michigan, Pennsylvania _____

8. Antartica, Australia, Asia _____

9. Panama, Honduras, El Salvedor _____

10. Canadian, Japaneese, Spanish _____

11. Mississippi, Amazon, Colarado _____

12. Beijing, Amsterdam, Tokeyo _____

Middle Grade Book of Language Tests

Find the errors. Re-write each headline **correctly**.

The Gazette, September 4, 1998

CHEF TRAPED IN RESAVOIR

13. _____

The Tribune, December 10, 2999

CURIUS VIRIS SWEEPS COUNTIE

16. _____

Morning News, July 4, 1999

Alliens Visit Five Cemataries

14. _____

The Evening News, February 10, 1997

Athalete Survives Food Poisening

17. _____

Daily Tidings, Saturday, April 3, 2000

JUDGE FINDS EMBEZLER GUILLTY

15. _____

The City Gazette, July 24, 2000

Counterfiet Perscriptions Siezed

18. _____

Leroy has some errors on his menu.
Write these words **correctly**.

19. _____

20. _____

21. _____

22. _____

23. _____

24. _____

25. _____

26. _____

27. _____

MENU

Appetizers
yoegurt finger snacks
celary sticks with ketchup dip

Main Course
onion-seeweed quiche
vegatable-orange juice stew
maceroni and gravy
sallmon-stuffed spider legs
poison-berry bisciuts

Desserts
shredded carrot sundays
cocanut-liver ice cream

Name _____

149

Find the misspelled word in each phrase. **Write it correctly.**

28. dinasaurs descending on the dormitory _____

29. miscellaneous llamas in jepardy _____

30. technically talented technisians _____

31. a carburator filled with chromosomes _____

32. not nearly enuf molasses _____

33. nine naughtty navigators _____

34. a detective's defectave parachute _____

35. a begger happily eating egg yolks _____

36. mathamatics equations to memorize _____

37. plenty of trouble for the villian _____

38. a police lieutenant checking a lisence _____

39. a strenuous holiday celabration _____

40. scientists examineing molecules _____

41. louzy weather every Saturday _____

42. horrably frightening lightning _____

43. ancient pyjamas from the attic _____

44. a perfactly charming rhinoceros _____

Find the errors in the chef's exclamation. **Write the words correctly.**

I've contrackted to have fourty pizzas prepared by eight o'clock for this outragous surprize party! Oh, this douwgh is too heavy! The distinguished guests will complane!

45. _____

46. _____

47. _____

48. _____

49. _____

50. _____

Middle Grade Book of Language Tests

Find the spelling errors. **Rewrite each sign's message correctly.**

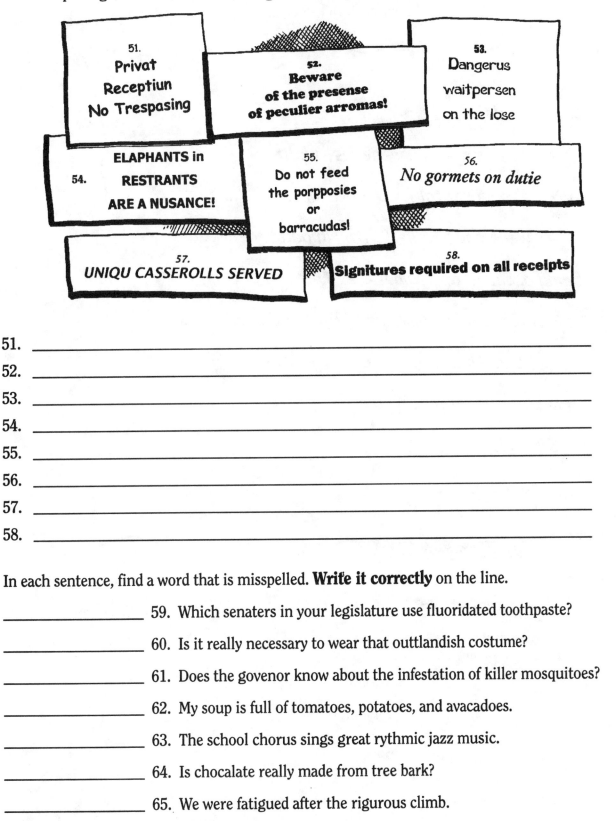

51. Privat Receptiun No Trespasing

52. Beware of the presense of peculier arromas!

53. Dangerus waitpersen on the lose

54. ELAPHANTS in RESTRANTS ARE A NUSANCE!

55. Do not feed the porpposies or barracudas!

56. No gormets on dutie

57. UNIQU CASSEROLLS SERVED

58. Signitures required on all receipts

51. _____

52. _____

53. _____

54. _____

55. _____

56. _____

57. _____

58. _____

In each sentence, find a word that is misspelled. **Write it correctly** on the line.

_____ 59. Which senaters in your legislature use fluoridated toothpaste?

_____ 60. Is it really necessary to wear that outtlandish costume?

_____ 61. Does the govenor know about the infestation of killer mosquitoes?

_____ 62. My soup is full of tomatoes, potatoes, and avacadoes.

_____ 63. The school chorus sings great rythmic jazz music.

_____ 64. Is chocalate really made from tree bark?

_____ 65. We were fatigued after the rigurous climb.

_____ 66. This medasin will cure your illness.

67–85. Correct the spelling in the letter and on the envelope. Cross out any misspelled words and write them correctly above the words. (Find 19 errors.)

Dear Freida,

We had a strange ocurrene last night

in the experimental food labratory. All the test

tubes were found filled with whiped creem. I am

being accuzed of neglagence. This is a puzling

mysterie, and it looks as if I am in some serius

troubble. This is not an exxaggeration!

Please contact my laywer.

Sincerly,

Chef Frankie

Chef Frankie S. Fricassee

Countie Jail

Jaynsville, Flordia

Freida Friendly

16 Ocen Bulevard

San Fransisco, Calafornia

STOP

KEEPING TRACK OF SKILLS

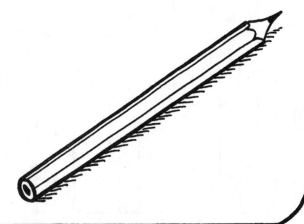

STUDENT PROGRESS RECORD — LANGUAGE SKILLS

Student Name _____

READING TESTS	SCORE	OF	COMMENTS & NEEDS
TEST DATE			
Test # 1 Word Meanings	of	50	
Test # 2 Literal Comprehension	of	40	
Test # 3 Inferential & Evaluative Comprehension	of	30	
Test # 4 Literature Skills	of	55	

WRITING TESTS	SCORE	OF	COMMENTS & NEEDS
TEST DATE			
Test # 1 Word Choice & Word Use	of	25	
Test # 2 Forms & Techniques	of	35	
Test # 3 Content & Organization	of	50	
Test # 4 Editing	of	50	
Test # 5 Writing Process	of	30	

GRAMMAR & USAGE TESTS	SCORE	OF	COMMENTS & NEEDS
TEST DATE			
Test # 1 Parts of Speech	of	90	
Test # 2 Sentences	of	50	
Test # 3 Phrases & Clauses	of	35	
Test # 4 Capitalization & Punctuation	of	40	
Test # 5 Language Usage	of	50	

VOCABULARY & WORD SKILLS TESTS	SCORE	OF	COMMENTS & NEEDS
TEST DATE			
Test # 1 Word Parts	of	80	
Test # 2 Vocabulary Word Meanings	of	60	
Test # 3 Confusing Words	of	55	

STUDY & RESEARCH SKILLS TESTS	SCORE	OF	COMMENTS & NEEDS
TEST DATE			
Test # 1 Dictionary & Encyclopedia Skills	of	30	
Test # 2 Reference & Information Skills	of	75	
Test # 3 Library Skills	of	50	
Test # 4 Study Skills	of	15	

SPELLING TESTS	SCORE	OF	COMMENTS & NEEDS
TEST DATE			
Test # 1 Rules & Rule Breakers	of	84	
Test # 2 Spelling with Word Parts	of	70	
Test # 3 Confusing & Tricky Words	of	50	
Test # 4 Correcting Spelling Errors	of	85	

Middle Grade Book of Language Tests

CLASS PROGRESS RECORD – LANGUAGE SKILLS
(Reading, Writing)

Class _____

Teacher _____

READING TESTS

TEST DATE	TEST	COMMENTS ABOUT RESULTS	SKILLS NEEDING RE-TEACHING
	Test # 1 Word Meanings		
	Test # 2 Literal Comprehension		
	Test # 3 Inferential & Evaluative Comprehension		
	Test # 4 Literature Skills		

WRITING TESTS

TEST DATE	TEST	COMMENTS ABOUT RESULTS	SKILLS NEEDING RE-TEACHING
	Test # 1 Word Choice & Word Use		
	Test # 2 Forms & Techniques		
	Test # 3 Content & Organization		
	Test # 4 Editing		
	Test # 5 Writing Process		

CLASS PROGRESS RECORD – LANGUAGE SKILLS

(Grammar & Usage, Vocabulary & Word Skills)

Class _____   Teacher _____

GRAMMAR & USAGE TESTS

TEST DATE	TEST	COMMENTS ABOUT RESULTS	SKILLS NEEDING RE-TEACHING
	Test # 1 Parts of Speech		
	Test # 2 Sentences		
	Test # 3 Capitalization & Punctuation		
	Test # 4 Language Usage		

VOCABULARY & WORD SKILLS TESTS

TEST DATE	TEST	COMMENTS ABOUT RESULTS	SKILLS NEEDING RE-TEACHING
	Test # 1 Word Parts		
	Test # 2 Vocabulary Word Meanings		
	Test # 3 Confusing Words		

Middle Grade Book of Language Tests

CLASS PROGRESS RECORD – LANGUAGE SKILLS

(Study & Research Skills, Spelling)

Class _____   Teacher _____

STUDY & RESEARCH SKILLS TESTS

TEST DATE	TEST	COMMENTS ABOUT RESULTS	SKILLS NEEDING RE-TEACHING
	Test # 1 Dictionary & Encyclopedia Skills		
	Test # 2 Reference & Information Skills		
	Test # 3 Library Skills		
	Test # 4 Study Skills		

SPELLING TESTS

TEST DATE	TEST	COMMENTS ABOUT RESULTS	SKILLS NEEDING RE-TEACHING
	Test # 1 Rules & Rule Breakers		
	Test # 2 Spelling with Word Parts		
	Test # 3 Confusing & Tricky Words		
	Test # 4 Correcting Spelling Errors		

GOOD SKILL SHARPENERS
FOR LANGUAGE ARTS

The tests in this book will identify student needs for practice, re-teaching or reinforcement of basic skills.

Once those areas of need are known, then what? You and your students need to find some good ways to strengthen those skills.

The BASIC/Not Boring Skills Series, published by Incentive Publications (www.incentivepublications.com), offers twenty books to sharpen basic skills at the middle grade level. Six of these books are full of language exercises in the areas of reading, writing, grammar and language usage, study and research, vocabulary and word skills, and spelling.

The pages of these books are student-friendly, clever, and challenging—guaranteed not to be boring! They cover a wide range of skills, including the skills assessed in this book of tests. A complete checklist of skills is available at the front of each book, complete with a reference list directing you to the precise pages for polishing those skills.

TEST IN THIS BOOK Middle Grade Book of Language Tests	Pages in this Book	You will find pages to sharpen skills in these locations from the BASIC/Not Boring Skills Series, published by Incentive Publications.
Reading Test # 1 **Word Meanings**	12–17	Gr. 6–8 Reading Comprehension Gr. 6–8 Words & Vocabulary
Reading Test # 2 **Literal Comprehension**	18–25	Gr. 6–8 Reading Comprehension Gr. 6–8 Study & Research Skills
Reading Test # 3 **Inferential & Evaluative Comprehension**	26–33	Gr. 6–8 Reading Comprehension Gr. 6–8 Study & Research Skills
Reading Test # 4 **Literature Skills**	34–39	Gr. 6–8 Reading Comprehension
Writing Test # 1 **Word Choice & Word Use**	42–45	Gr. 6–8 Writing
Writing Test # 2 **Forms & Techniques**	46–51	Gr. 6–8 Writing
Writing Test # 3 **Content & Organization**	52–57	Gr. 6–8 Writing
Writing Test # 4 **Editing**	58–63	Gr. 6–8 Writing Gr. 6–8 Grammar & Usage
Writing Test # 5 **Writing Process**	64–71	Gr. 6–8 Writing

(continued on next page)

TEST IN THIS BOOK Middle Grade Book of Language Tests	Pages in this Book	You will find pages to sharpen skills in these locations from the BASIC/Not Boring Skills Series, published by Incentive Publications.
Grammar & Usage Test # 1 **Parts of Speech**	75–81	Gr. 6–8 Grammar & Usage
Grammar & Usage Test # 2 **Sentences**	82–85	Gr. 6–8 Grammar & Usage
Grammar & Usage Test # 3 **Phrases & Clauses**	86–89	Gr. 6–8 Grammar & Usage
Grammar & Usage Test # 4 **Capitalization & Punctuation**	90–93	Gr. 6–8 Grammar & Usage Gr. 6–8 Writing
Grammar & Usage Test # 5 **Language Usage**	94–97	Gr. 6–8 Grammar & Usage
Vocabulary & Word Skills Test # 1 **Word Parts**	100–103	Gr. 6–8 Words & Vocabulary Gr. 6–8 Spelling
Vocabulary & Word Skills Test # 2 **Vocabulary Word Meanings**	104–109	Gr. 6–8 Words & Vocabulary Gr. 6–8 Spelling
Vocabulary & Word Skills Test #3 **Confusing Words**	110–113	Gr. 6–8 Words & Vocabulary Gr. 6–8 Spelling
Study & Research Skills Test # 1 **Dictionary & Encyclopedia Skills**	116–119	Gr. 6–8 Study & Research Skills
Study & Research Skills Test # 2 **Reference & Information Skills**	120–125	Gr. 6–8 Study & Research Skills Gr. 6–8 Reading Comprehension
Study & Research Skills Test # 3 **Library Skills**	126–129	Gr. 6–8 Study & Research Skills
Study & Research Skills Test # 4 **Study Skills**	130–133	Gr. 6–8 Study & Research Skills
Spelling Test # 1 **Rules & Rule Breakers**	136–139	Gr. 6–8 Spelling
Spelling Test # 2 **Spelling with Word Parts**	140–143	Gr. 6–8 Spelling
Spelling Test # 3 **Confusing & Tricky Words**	144–147	Gr. 6–8 Spelling
Spelling Test # 4 **Correcting Spelling Errors**	148–152	Gr. 6–8 Spelling Gr. 6–8 Writing

SCORING GUIDES & ANSWER KEYS

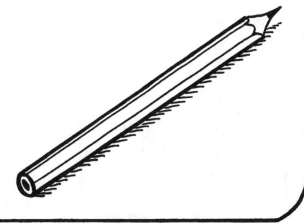

READING TESTS ANSWER KEY

Word Meanings (Test on pages 12)

1. d	18. c	35. work
2. c	19. b	36. cut
3. b	20. b	37. heat
4. b	21. c	38. foot
5. c	22. a	39. break
6. b	23. c	40. touch
7. b	24. b	41. words
8. d	25. a	42. look-see
9. a	26. c	43. hand
10. command	27. a	44. c
11. courage	28. c	45. b
12. probe	29. b	46. H
13. pursuit	30. a	47. C
14. precarious	31. b	48. B
15. extreme (or radical)	32. carry	49. F
16. relish	33. sleep	50. D
17. succumb	34. hang	

Literal Comprehension (Test on page 18)

1. c	17. Angelino's	*33–40. Check student drawings to see that the following is done accurately:*
2. 4	18. Pizza Heaven and Papa G's	
3. b	19. Angelino's (or www.angelino.com)	33. frog has a 3-digit number greater than 116
4. when the wave picks up the board	20. nothing	34. cat has a 2-digit number with no digits smaller than 5
5. the wall of vertical face	21. a	
6. wipe out	22. 3, 9	35. glasses have been drawn on the rat
7. nothing	23. 5, 7, 10 (4 and 6 are optional)	36. a grape has been drawn for the pig
8. b	24. 2, 1, 5, 4, 3, 6	
9. c	25. February 9, 1992	37. a cricket has been drawn for the dog
10. permanent eyeliner or lip color	26. July 27, 2000	38. a hat has been drawn on the frog
11. c	27. banana eating	
12. c	28. a	39. a grape has been drawn for the rat
13. 2	29. 52	
14. 2	30. c	40. a watermelon seed has been drawn for the cat
15. chicken, calzone	31. b	
16. pizzas can be baked at home	32. 5, 3, 2, 4, 1	

Middle Grade Book of Language Tests

READING TESTS ANSWER KEY

Inferential & Evaluative Comprehension (Test on page 26)

1. c
2. b
3. c
4. b
5. c
6. a
7. O
8. F
9. F
10. O
11. F
12. Because of that, more people are learning to climb.
13. b
14. b
15. c
16. c
17. yes
18. a
19. b
20. c
21. b
22. b
23. b
24. c
25. 3, 4 (2 is optional)
26. c
27. 120
28. 116
29. 118
30. Matt

Literature Skills (Test on page 32)

1. the backyard
2. Latitia
3. neighborhood kids, soccer team, 8th grade class (town is optional)
4. d
5. c
6. b
7. a, d, e
8. poem
9. joke
10. biography
11. news report
12. advertisement
13. food
14. c
15. b
16. a, a, b, b
17. a
18. poem D, line 4
19. RTH or R
20. I
21. S
22. PN
23. H
24. I
25. A
26. PN
27. P
28. RP
29. M
30. P
31. P
32. A
33. S
34. R
35. Q
36. P
37. There are several possibilities. Students should choose three contrasting pairs of words (or whole lines) such as these:
   dreaded—looked forward to
   glad—yet scared
   hate—love
   mixed blessings
   hard—fun
   new—old
   nervous—excited
38. a
39. b
40. b
41. b
42. There are several possibilities. Students should name two:
   great sales
   latest hot clothing and equipment
   the coolest salespersons
   you'll love the awesome free stickers and posters
   extremely wild T-shirt
   They cater to kids
   you feel real important as a customer
43. crowned him
44. keep a lid on
45. driving her up the wall
46. was out in the cold
47. lost her marbles
   or, blown her top
   or, lost her cool
   or, was fit to be tied
   or, went totally bananas
48. mood
49. tone
50. theme
51. flashback
52. setting
53. conflict
54. plot
55. climax

Middle Grade Book of Language Tests

WRITING TESTS ANSWER KEY

Word Choice & Word Use (Test on page 42)

1. b
2. a
3. c
4. c
5. d
6. c
7. c, e, g, h (optional: b)
8. answers will vary: something like *grumpy*
9. answers will vary: something like *slow* or *lazy*
10. b
11. c
12. a
13. c
14. Cross out: *who was kind of like my grandfather* or *old and kind of*; *together*
15. Cross out: *of the day*
16. Cross out: *In my opinion* or *I think*; *also* or *as well*
17. Cross out: *fearful*; *15-year-old*
18. Answers may vary somewhat: (Student does not have to get every one of these) Circle: *deviously, illegally,* (or the whole last sentence)
19. Answers may vary somewhat: (Student does not have to get every one of these—two or more are acceptable) Circle: *It makes your pulse race with excitement; tells your happy feet to move; clever rhymes; fetching rhythms; grab the listener's ear*
20. b
21. a
22. a
23. c
24. b
25. c

Forms & Techniques (Test on page 46)

1. A, D, I (possibly K)
2. B, J
3. C, F
4. B, H, K (possibly A)
5. E, G
6. A
7. c
8. c
9. a
10. d
11. b
12. c
13. e
14. G, M
15. C, L (possibly N)
16. D, J
17. B, E
18. A, O
19. F, H, I (possibly N)
20. N
21. K
22. a, c
23. 7, 8, 9, 10, 11, 12, 13, 14, 15, (possibly 16)
24. a
25. c
26. Yellow
27. any 5 of these: steps, throwing, dashes, splashes, drips, wraps, reaches
28. answers will vary
29. 4 (or 5)
30. a, d, e, f
31. 1 (or 2)
32. b, d
33. a
34. c
35. d

Middle Grade Book of Language Tests
Copyright ©2001 by Incentive Publications, Inc., Nashville, TN.

WRITING TESTS ANSWER KEY

Content & Organization (Test on page 52)

> To the adult:
> The ten writing tasks will have varied answers. Assign 1–5 points for each, depending upon how well the student followed the directions, and how thoroughly the work is done. Do not emphasize spelling, punctuation, and capitalization too much in scoring, as it will obscure attention to the skills being examined in each task.

Editing (Test on page 58)

To the adult:
Many of the ten editing tasks will have varied answers. Assign 1–5 points for each, depending upon how well the student followed the directions, and how thoroughly the work is done. Do not emphasize spelling, punctuation, and capitalization too much in scoring, except for in Task # 10, as it will obscure attention to the skills being examined in each task.

Answers are given below only for those tasks that clearly have right answers:

Task # 2
Answers will vary. Accept any answer that makes the meaning clear. Possibly:
   a. While driving her motorcycle, the science teacher whistled to her dog.
   b. While I was riding my bike in the morning, the sun was getting hot.
   c. While we were entertaining the Johnson family for lunch, my sister told jokes.

Task # 3
   a. 3, 1, 4, 2, 5
   b. 2, 1, 5, 4, 3

Task # 4
   1. Cross out: *these, totally*
   2. Cross out: *three shapes, three-sided, round*
   3. Cross out: *In my opinion* OR *I think that; not* OR *never*

Task # 10
Corrected letter is as follows:

January 15, 2001

Dear Editor,

The situation with the parking in the downtown area is abominable! Why doesn't the city council do something about this? They are allowing more and more development, yet the parking is not growing to keep up with the traffic. It is getting so that a person cannot stop to shop in the plaza area any longer. To make matters worse, the city has just restricted 15 parking spaces in the busiest area. According to the sign, these are now reserved for city vehicles. City administrators: are you listening? Your citizens are not happy about this.

Sincerely,

Annoyed Andrew

WRITING PROCESS SCORING GUIDE

TRAIT	SCORE OF 5	SCORE OF 3	SCORE OF 1
CONTENT	• The writing is very clear and focused. • The main ideas and purpose stand out clearly. • Main ideas are well-supported with details and examples. • All details are relevant to the main idea. • The ideas have some freshness and insight. • The ideas fit the purpose and audience well. • The paper is interesting and holds the reader's attention.	• The writing is mostly clear and focused. • The main ideas and purpose are mostly clear. • Details and examples are used but may be somewhat limited or repetitive. • Most details are relevant to the main idea. • Some details may be off the topic. • Some ideas and details are fresh; others are ordinary. • The paper is interesting to some degree. • The ideas and content are less than precisely right for the audience and purpose.	• The writing lacks clarity and focus. • It is hard to identify the main idea. • The purpose of the writing is not evident. • Details are few, not relevant, or repetitive. • Ideas or details have little sparkle or appeal to hold the reader's attention. • The paper has not developed an idea well.
WORD CHOICE	• Writer has used strong, specific, colorful, effective, and varied words. • Words are used well to convey the ideas. • Words are well chosen to fit the content, audience, and purpose. • Writer has chosen fresh, unusual words, and/or has used words/phrases in an unusual way. • Writer has made use of figurative language, and words/phrases that create images.	• Writer has used some specific and effective words. • A good use of colorful, unusual words is attempted, but limited or overdone. • The words succeed at conveying main ideas. • The writer uses words in fresh ways sometimes, but not consistently. • The word choice is mostly suited to the content, audience, and purpose.	• There is a limited use of specific, effective, or colorful words. • Some words chosen are imprecise, misused, or repetitive. • The words do not suit the content, purpose, or audience well. • The words do not succeed at conveying the main ideas.
SENTENCES	• Sentences have a pleasing and natural flow. • When read aloud, sentences and ideas flow along smoothly from one to another. • Transitions between sentences are smooth and natural. • Sentences have varied length, structure, sound, and rhythm. • The structure of sentences focuses reader's attention on the main idea and key details. • The sentence sound and variety make the reading enjoyable. • If the writer uses dialogue, it is used correctly and effectively.	• Most of the sentences have a natural flow. • When read aloud, some sentences have a "less than fluid" sound. • Some or all transitions are awkward or repetitive. • There is some variety in sentence length, structure, sound, and rhythm; but some patterns are repetitive. • The sentences convey the main idea and details, but without much craftsmanship. • If the writer uses dialogue, it is somewhat less than fluid or effective.	• Most sentences are not fluid. • When read aloud, the writing sounds awkward or uneven. Some of the paper is confusing to read. • Transitions are not effective. • There is little variety in sentence length, structure, sound, or rhythm. • There may be incomplete or run-on sentences. • The sentence structure gets in the way of conveying content, purpose, and meaning.

A score of 4 may be given for papers that fall between 3 and 5 on a trait. A score of 2 may be given for papers that fall between 1 and 3.

Middle Grade Book of Language Tests

WRITING PROCESS SCORING GUIDE

TRAIT	SCORE OF 5	SCORE OF 3	SCORE OF 1
ORGANIZATION	• The organization of the piece allows the main ideas and key details to be conveyed well. • The piece has a compelling beginning that catches the attention of the reader. • Ideas are developed in a clear, interesting sequence. • The piece moves along from one idea, sentence, or paragraph to another in a manner that is smooth and useful to develop the meaning. • The piece has a compelling ending that ties up the idea well and leaves the reader feeling pleased.	• Organization is recognizable, but weak or inconsistent in some places. • For the most part, the organization of the piece allows the main ideas and key details to be conveyed. • The structure seems somewhat ordinary, lacking flavor or originality. • The piece has a beginning that is not particularly inviting to the reader or not well-developed. • Some of the sequencing is confusing. • The piece does not always move along smoothly or clearly from one idea, sentence, or paragraph to another. • The piece has a clear ending, but it is somewhat dull or underdeveloped, or does not adequately tie up the piece.	• The piece lacks clear organization. • For the most part, the lack of good organization gets in the way of the conveyance of the main ideas and key details. • The piece does not have a clear beginning or ending. • Ideas are not developed in any clear sequence, or the sequence is distracting. • The piece does not move along smoothly from one sentence or paragraph to another. • Important ideas or details seem to be missing or out of place. • The piece leaves the reader feeling confused.
VOICE	• The writer has left a personal stamp on the piece. A reader knows there is a person behind the writing. • It is clear that the writer knows what audience and purpose he/she is reaching. • The writer engages the audience. • The writer shows passion, commitment, originality, and honesty in conveying the message. • The voice used (level of personal closeness) is appropriate for the purpose of the piece.	• The writer has left a personal stamp on the piece, but this is not as strong or consistent as it might be. The reader is not always sure of the writer's presence. • It is not always clear that the writer knows his/her audience and purpose. • The writer engages the audience some, but not all of the time. • The writer shows some passion, commitment, originality, and honesty in conveying the message, but this is inconsistent.	• The writer has not left any personal stamp on the piece. The writing feels detached. • There is little sense that the writer is speaking to the audience or clearly knows the purpose of the writing. • There is little or no engagement of the audience. • The writer shows little or no passion, commitment, originality, and honesty in conveying the message.
CONVENTIONS	• There is clear control of capitalization, punctuation, spelling, and paragraphing. • There is consistent use of correct grammar and language usage. • The strong use of conventions strengthens the communication of the work's meaning. • The piece needs little editing/revision.	• There is some control of capitalization, punctuation, spelling, and paragraphing. • There is inconsistent use of correct grammar and language usage. • The uneven use of conventions sometimes interferes with the meaning. • The piece needs much editing/revision.	• There is poor control of capitalization, punctuation, spelling, and paragraphing. • There is a lack of correct grammar and language usage. • Poor use of conventions obscures meaning. • There are multiple errors; the piece needs extensive editing/revision.

A score of 4 may be given for papers that fall between 3 and 5 on a trait. A score of 2 may be given for papers that fall between 1 and 3.

Middle Grade Book of Language Tests

GRAMMAR & USAGE TESTS ANSWER KEY

Parts of Speech (Test on page 75)

1. AJ
2. AJ
3. N
4. V
5. AD
6. AJ
7. N
8. AJ
9. N
10. N
11. V
12. AD
13. AD
14. N
15. moan, foghorn, tonight
16. heard, sounds
17. never, tonight
18. Grandville, dive, team, Saturday, south, atlantic, ocean
19. captain, ship, waters
20. Her, it, yours
21. She, they, there, her, its
22. businesses
23. knives
24. pianos
25. geese
26. sisters-in-law
27. children
28. mouse
29. moose
30. city
31. pastry
32. ax or axe
33. accident
34. monkeys' surfboards
35. girls' swimsuits
36. swimmer's goggles
37. lifeguards' appetites
38. octopus's tentacles
39. Mr. Zax's pet jellyfish
40. Spike's raft
41. We
42. mine
43. Others
44. Which
45. those
46. b
47. a
48. a
49. b
50. c
51. c
52. b
53. b
54. a
55. c
56. L
57. A
58. L
59. T
60. I
61. I
62. T
63. thought
64. seems
65. sailed, dashed, escaped, signed
66. was, write, send, ate, was, find
67. find, come, built, rode, fell, flew, wrote
68. swam
69. dove
70. took
71. brought
72. worry
73. go
74. break
75. write
76. six, mischievous, Mrs. O'Grady's, pet
77. totally, promptly
78. kids
79. dumped
80. b
81. c
82. a
83. c
84. B
85. A, C, E, G
86. F, H, I
87. B, D
88. burned
89. eating
90. D

Sentences (Test on page 82)

1. R
2. F
3. C
4. F
5. C
6. C, H
7. A, F
8. D, E (A and F are optional)
9. B, G
10. S
11. C
12. CX
13. C
14. CX
15. octopus
16. submarines
17. volcanoes
18. Who
19. Look
20. happened
21. reminded
22. try
23. You
24. You
25. Seven fierce pirates
26. My new underwater camera and flippers
27. The long blue whale, which eats millions of shrimp
28. A prickly sea urchin
29. 26
30. slept
31. are eating fresh fish tonight
32. Would go sailing during a hurricane
33. should never put a sea cucumber in a salad
34. inflates itself and makes itself look scary
35. 34
36. food (whales is optional)
37. monster
38. slimy
39. delicious
40. because
41. whenever
42. after
43. since
44. but
45. although
46. or
47. answers will vary
48. answers will vary
49. answers will vary; possibly: While I was sailing my boat, a fish jumped up and bit me.
50. answers will vary; possibly: While listening to the radio, I heard about a diver who got cornered by a shark.

Middle Grade Book of Language Tests

GRAMMAR & USAGE TESTS ANSWER KEY

Phrases & Clauses (Test on page 86)

1–6. 1, 3, 4, 5, 6 have misplaced or dangling modifiers
9. a lifeguard
10. the world's largest reef
11. the largest snail in the world
12. a floating colony of jellyfish
13. A, D, F, G, J
14. D, G, I, J
15. C, E, F
16. B, H
17. trying
18. on
19. Steering
20. to talk
21. B
22. D
23. B
24. D
25. ADJ
26. N
27. ADV
28. N
29. ADV
30. ADV
31. ADJ
32. Lolly
33. class
34. B, C, D
35. A, C

Capitalization & Punctuation (Test on page 90)

1–18. The errors in the letter are:
Capital letters needed on *June, Dear, Rita, Sincerely;*
Commas needed after *16, Rita, Sincerely;*
The errors in the envelope are:
Capitals needed on *Leroy, Leroux, West, End, Ave, Cheesetown, Vermin, Boulevard, Rodentville;*
Commas needed after *Cheesetown, Rodentville*
19. Spanish, Catholic, University, Officer, Wiley, New, England, Captain, Hook, Grand, Canyon, Valentine's, Day, Golden, Gate, Bridge, Aunt, Gerta, Indian, Ocean, Titanic, Easter
20. Circle: big, dipper, zuma, beach
21. B, C
22. B, C
23. A, D
24. D, E, G, H, I
25. won't, aren't, I'm, you're, they'll, don't, can't, they're
26. C, E, F (D optional)
27. A, D, E, F, G
28. thirty-two, mother-in-law, well-known, one-half, up-to-the-minute report
29. b
30. a
31. c
32. c
33. a
34–40. Correct capitalization and punctuation will be:
34. apostrophe in *here's*; no capital on *sea*
35. comma after *summer*; capitals on *liberty, new* and *york*; semicolon after *york* (or period, with capital on *It*)
36. capitals on *nine* and *ocean*, no capital on *sister*, period after *ocean*
37. capitals on *do* and *bay*, no capital on *lobsters*, question mark at end
38. no dash after *storm* (instead: parentheses around *it lasted four hours*), no colon
39. no capital on *island*, no commas in the sentence
40. apostrophe in *Spikes*, colon in *3:15*, no capital on *afternoon*

Middle Grade Book of Language Tests

GRAMMAR & USAGE TESTS ANSWER KEY

Language Usage (Test on page 94)

1. eat
2. hit
3. spread
4. surfs
5. fall
6. have
7. give
8. thinks
9. their
10. their
11. it
12. their
13. Who
14. who
15. Whoever
16. whom
17. whomever
18. b
19. d
20. us
21. we
22. them
23. her
24. She
25. her and them

26. him and me
27. A, C, F, G, I
28. *raise* instead of *rise*
29. *well* instead of *good*
30. *have* instead of *of*
31. *lay* instead of *laid*
32. *rise* instead or *raise*
33. *set* instead of *sit*
34. *good* instead of *well*
35. cross out *he*
36. *sit* instead of *set*
37. *teach* instead of *learn*
38. *let* instead of *leave*
39. *May* instead of *Can*
40. *Lain* instead of *laid*
41. *well* instead of *good*
42. *lay* instead of *lie*
43. D, F, I, J, K
44. I (circle *Spike*)
45. D (circle *snorkel*)
46. D (circle *diver*)
47. I (circle *boyfriend*)
48. I (circle *friend*)
49. D (circle *chowder*)
50. I (circle *you*)

Middle Grade Book of Language Tests
Copyright ©2001 by Incentive Publications, Inc., Nashville, TN.

VOCABULARY & WORD SKILLS TESTS ANSWER KEY

Word Parts (Test on page 100)

1. maximum
2. transmit
3. antidote
4. improper
5. malpractice
6. universe
7. subnormal
8. reorganize
9. supersonic
10. prepare
11. exit
12. hemisphere
13. il
14. anti
15. quadr
16. ex
17. auto
18. mis
19. kilo
20. dis or mis
21. co
22. hepta
23. hyper
24. in
25. trans
26. a or im
27. post
28. semi
29. terrorist (or Canadian)
30. hopeless
31. dangerous
32. Canadian
33. edible
34. wooden
35. backwards
36. clarity
37. foolish
38. magnify
39. ical
40. y
41. less
42. ward
43. or
44. en
45. ish or like
46. lets
47. en
48. gar
49. ish
50. ize
51. ous
52. ent
53. altitude
54. projectile
55. auditorium
56. tactile
57. gravity
58. applaud
59. translucent
60. laboratory
61. suspend
62. chronological
63. journal
64. torture
65. dynamite
66. synonym
67. astronomy
68. dormitory
69. geology or geography
70. unbendable or inflexible
71. governor
72. supernatural
73. ascend
74. election
75. tenderly
76. terrorist
77. subtract, perilous, octopus, oceanography
78. superjet, boycott, hurricane, friendly, subconscious
79. sailor, transatlantic, forecast, megaphone
80. hyperactive, nonsense

Middle Grade Book of Language Tests

VOCABULARY & WORD SKILLS TESTS ANSWER KEY

Vocabulary Word Meanings (Test on page 104)

1. yes
2. no
3. yes
4. no
5. yes
6. yes
7. no
8. no
9. no
10. yes
11. yes
12. no
13. treasure it
14. brush it
15. eat it
16. feed it
17. put it on a salad
18. in a movie
19. in your body
20. in jail
21. waiting in a medicine cabinet
22. a query
23. clavicle
24. your teeth
25. water
26. b
27. a
28. c
29. d
30. c
31. a
32. b
33. b
34. sunset
35. gossip
36. c
37. c
38. maelstrom
39. arrogant
40. goring
41. bickered
42. churlish
43. lethargic
44. boorish
45. thrilling
46. abominable
47. boisterous or impatient or maelstrom or wild or frothy or shrieking
48. adore
49. eclipse
50. brave
51. gloating
52. shuddering
53. lumbering
54. Furious
55. sopping
56. shriek
57. court
58. track
59. radius
60. Answers will vary. Possibilities: covering; skin of fish or reptile; instrument for measuring weight; series of musical notes; to climb

Confusing Words (Test on page 110)

1. biannual
2. vigorous
3. imminent
4. avert
5. defective
6. persecuting
7. instructing
8. assure
9. except
10. affect
11. adept
12. complaints
13. college
14. advice
15. insurance
16. endangered
17. acute
18. novice
19. rejected
20. circumference
21. bald
22. chance
23. ceiling
24. quarts
25. crews
26. hare or hair or air
27. rain or rein
28. instance
29. odd
30. navel
31. size
32. by, assistants
33. your, frees
34. caught, to
35. no, fined
36. patience, wait
37. fare, cents
38. minors, allowed
39. close, weather
40. wrapped, waist
41. c
42. k
43. l
44. e
45. a
46. h
47. j
48. g
49. b
50. trip
51. include
52. angry
53. rancid
54. flurries
55. selfish

Middle Grade Book of Language Tests

STUDY & RESEARCH SKILLS TESTS ANSWER KEY

Dictionary & Encyclopedia Skills (Test on page 116)

1. 3, 4, 5, 2, 1
2. b
3. a
4. c
5. 5, 1, 3, 6, 4, 2
6. 2, 3, 5, 1, 4
7. 4, 1, 2, 5, 3, 7, 6
8. comedian
9. monotony, monopoly, monk
10. humanoid, hush-hush
11. elastic; Einstein, Albert; Eiffel Tower
12. psoriasis, shingles
13. Madison, James; magnetism; mahogany; marsupial
14. hibernation, hysteria
15. refracted
16. b, c, e
17. electricity or static
18. *Titanic*
19. diseases or germs
20. Eiffel
21. personally
22. pervasive, pesky, petite
23. pestle, petition
24. pestilence, pestle, petition, petrify
25. French
26. pesto, petit fours
27. pet peeve
28. pessimism
29. pester
30. pestilence

Reference & Information Skills (Test on page 120)

1. thesaurus
2. atlas
3. book of quotations
4. dictionary
5. encyclopedia
6. biographical dictionary
7. timeline
8. almanac
9. book of records
10. geographical dictionary
11–34: Much of this information can be found on the Internet. You may allow J as an answer for most items.
11. D
12. D
13. H or B
14. O
15. A or G
16. J or K
17. E
18. I
19. J or N
20. D
21. J or K
22. J or B
23. J or E
24. J or E
25. J or L
26. C
27. J
28. O
29. J
30. B or J
31. J
32. J or K
33. H
34. F
35. e
36. c
37. f
38. d
39. a
40. b
41. 2, 3
42. 46–67
43. 1
44. 54–56
45. 84
46. 2
47. 34 (pages 12–45)
48. 62–67
49. 93–99
50. 54–56
51. 70–77
52. 68–99
53. 48–53, 62–67
54. 26–31, 18–25, 40–45, 32–39
55. a, b (c optional)
56. b, c
57. d
58. c
59. east
60. yes
61. 7
62. doughnut holes
63. Missing Doughnut Holes
64. Money Drop, Mysterious Scents
65. March, May, November
66. 3
67. suspicious noises
68. 4
69. 3
70. 40
71. 1991
72. 1996
73. 10
74. 1994–1997
75. about 55

Middle Grade Book of Language Tests

STUDY & RESEARCH SKILLS TESTS ANSWER KEY

Library Skills (Test on page 126)

1. a	17. a	35. 500
2. b	18. NY	36. 200
3. c	19. A Hog on Ice	37. 700
4. c	20. Tom Funk	38. 600
5. a	21. c	39. 300
6. a	22. Aubrey Wrapp	40. 700
7. b	23. Lost in Deep Space	41. 2, 1, 3, 5, 4, 6
8. b	24. 1988	42. a
9. C. Sports, Inc.	25. 400	43. e
10. yes	26. 800	44. l
11. Hilarious Sports Blunders	27. 100	45. f
	28. 800	46. j
12. Hugh Molhalland	29. 500	47. b
13. Strange Sights in the Night Sky	30. 200	48. c
	31. 700	49. g
14. 1999	32. 900	50. n
15. Julia Lynton	33. 900	
16. 244	34. 700	

Study Skills (Test on page 130)

1. a, b, d, e, f, g, j
2. broke in
3. 12
4. bathtub toys
5. Answers will vary: Mice parachuted into a restaurant at the dinner hour.
6. A, B, C, D, F, G, H
7. b
8. Answers will vary: Something like: Money Bundles Left in City Parks
9. Answers will vary: Something like: City Hall Vanishes
10. Answers will vary: Something like: Ant Farm Disappears
11. I B
12. V B
13. IV C
14. III
15. II A

SPELLING TESTS ANSWER KEY

Rules & Rule Breakers (Test on page 136)

1. friend
2. achieve
3. believe
4. deceit
5. retrieve
6. sleigh
7. grief
8. neighbor
9. deceive
10. conceited
11. freight
12. perceive
13. ceiling
14. receipt
15. vein
16. sincerely
17. shiny
18. famous
19. marriage
20. hottest
21. shopping
22. business
23. greivus
24. getto
25. faraoh
26. jiant
27. nashing
28. rubarb
29. knaughty
30. fysics
31. rymes
32. zylophone
33. sider
34. sissors
35. rodeos
36. foxes
37. mosquitoes
38. donkeys
39. brothers-in-law
40. teeth
41. holidays
42. dragonflies
43. mouse
44. zero
45. loaf
46. genius
47. tomato
48. city
49. halo
50. goose
51. ballot
52. caterpillar
53. embarrassed
54. bizarre
55. parallel
56. opossum
57. B
58. A
59. C
60. froze
61. caught
62. fried
63. shone
64. slept
65. brought
66. bubblgum
67. roomate
68. hitchiker
69. horsfly
70. headdache
71. sholace
72. baskettball
73. homwork
74. fircracker
75. ancient
76. counterfeit
77. caffeine
78. wholly
79. courageous
80. financier
81. pastime
82. truly
83. altos
84. forfeit

Spelling with Word Parts (Test on page 140)

1–30: These are the incorrect words, spelled correctly:

5. interstate
6. antibacterial
11. energize
14. actor
15. horrific
16. treacherous
18. hopeful
20. circular
21. dissection
22. microscopic
24. unresponsive
27. distasteful
30. disagreeable
31. ekxtractions
32. unbeleivably
33. unstabel
34. inshurance
35. descussion
36. disappear
37. surprising
38. difference
39. favorable
40. accidental
41. troublesome
42. invisible
43. frequently
44. reflection
45. hoping
46. worked
47. cracked
48. worried
49. called
50. mumbled
51. hummed
52. swallowed
53. advantage
54. knowledge
55. criticize
56. dangerous
57. insurance
58. prevention
59. occasion
60. vessel
61. fragile
62. selfish, cowardice, punitive, realist
63. juvenile, florist
64. abolish, exercise, infantile, fragile
65. nuisance, absence, presence
66. dangerous, marvelous, circus, focus, vicious
67. radical, quarrel, brutal
68. dependent, important, elegant, migrant
69. prevention, occasion, fortune, decision, vacation
70. impossible, reversible, noticeable, ventricle, level, rural

Middle Grade Book of Language Tests

SPELLING TESTS ANSWER KEY

Confusing & Tricky Words (Test on page 144)

1. wimper, Lincon, rubarb, brige, rythm, forcast, restle
2. spaghetti
3. mosquito
4. kindergarten
5. doughnut
6. diamond
7. chauffeur
8. carousel
9. eo
10. ea
11. au
12. ue
13. oi
14. ui
15. ea
16. ou
17. hygiene
18. thesaurus
19. terrain
20. camouflage
21. unique, fraud, plausible
22. hoarse, chaos
23. cauliflower, Eisenhower, dinosaur
24. bias
25. yes
26. no
27. no
28. stalactite
29. adapting
30. hysterical
31. insurance
32. compliments
33. altogether
34. Albuquerque
35. peculiarities
36. sousaphone
37. psychiatrist
38. tattoo
39. anemone
40. staccato
41. circumstances
42. catastrophe
43. corduroy
44. suspiscious
45. absourb
46. protien
47. noticable
48. amatur
49. immingrant
50. Flordia

Correcting Spelling Errors (Test on page 148)

1. Nations
2. Caribbean
3. Eisenhower
4. Chicago
5. Halloween
6. Belgium
7. Missouri
8. Antarctica
9. El Salvador
10. Japanese
11. Colorado
12. Tokyo
13. Chef Trapped in Reservoir
14. Aliens Visit Five Cemeteries
15. Judge Finds Embezzler Guilty
16. Curious Virus Sweeps County
17. Athlete Survives Food Poisoning
18. Counterfeit Prescriptions Seized

19–27: The following words have been spelled incorrectly on the menu. Correct spellings are:
yogurt
celery
seaweed
vegetable
macaroni
salmon
biscuits
sundaes
coconut

28. dinosaurs
29. jeopardy
30. technicians
31. carburetor
32. enough
33. naughty
34. defective
35. beggar
36. mathematics
37. villain
38. license
39. celebration
40. examining
41. lousy
42. horribly
43. pajamas
44. perfectly

45–50: The following words have been spelled wrong in the chef's quote. Correct spellings are:
contracted
forty
outrageous
surprise
dough
complain

51. Private Reception No Trespassing
52. Beware of the presence of peculiar aromas
53. Dangerous waitperson on the loose
54. Elephants in Restaurants are a Nuisance!
55. Do Not Feed the Porpoises or Barracudas!
56. No gourmets on duty
57. Unique Casseroles Served
58. Signatures required on all receipts
59. Senators
60. outlandish
61. governor
62. avocados
63. rhythmic
64. chocolate
65. rigorous
66. medicine

67–85: The following words are spelled incorrectly on the letter. Correct spellings are as follows:
occurrence
laboratory
whipped
cream
accused
negligence
puzzling
mystery
serious
trouble
exaggeration
lawyer
Sincerely

The following words are spelled wrong on the envelope. Correct spellings are as follows:
County
Florida
Ocean
Boulevard
Francisco
California

Middle Grade Book of Language Tests